CW00496991

THE ONLY CHATGPT
PROMPTS BOOK
YOU'LL EVER NEED

Discover How To Craft Clear And Effective Prompts For
Maximum Impact Through
Prompt Engineering Techniques

GPT PENGUIN

YOUR FREE GIFT

As a way of saying thanks for your purchase, I'm giving away the following ChatGPT Bonus Files for **FREE** to my readers!

To get instant access just visit: gptpenguin.com

Inside the bonus files you will discover:

- Printable Income Tracker
- Simple Guide To Build Wealth From Home
- 33 Different Ways You Can Make Money Online
- Step-By-Step Guide On How To Get Started With ChatGPT

Simply scan this QR code below with your camera to download your free bonuses:

CONTENTS

BONUS CHAPTERS

INTRODUCTION

> "Any sufficiently advanced technology is indistinguishable
> from magic."
> — *Arthur C. Clarke*

You're on the hunt for the secret to unlocking the full potential of ChatGPT, seeking to transform good responses into truly exceptional ones that drive success. There's no shortage of books, articles, and tips offering formulas and "cheat codes" to generate satisfactory results. But these resources often scratch the surface, cater to specific use cases, or are formulaic, requiring constant reference and lacking a cohesive theory that can be applied universally.

In the long run, memorizing specific implementations and adapting them to various situations isn't practical or scalable. What you need is a deep understanding of the principles and techniques used by experts to unleash the true power of ChatGPT. That's where this book comes in.

As a software integration consultant with over a decade of experience exploring technology and its practical applications across various industries. My fascination with earlier GPT models from OpenAI evolved into an obsession with ChatGPT, leading me to spend countless hours reading, experimenting, and refining my techniques. Through practice, I've developed a set of proprietary techniques based on a consistent set of fundamentals that will elevate your prompting game and unlock the full potential of ChatGPT.

By mastering these principles, you'll no longer need to memorize formulas or rely on external resources. Instead, you'll be equipped with the knowledge to craft the right prompt at the right time, tailoring ChatGPT's responses to your unique needs and situations.

These principles have transformed the lives and techniques of those I've trained, helping them attain 10X results or more. The philosophy at the heart of these principles is simple, yet effective. This book will unveil the same training, equipping you with the philosophy, approach, and practical skills you need to become an advanced ChatGPT user.

As AI continues to permeate every aspect of our lives, early adopters stand to reap the greatest rewards. By mastering ChatGPT now, you'll gain a competitive edge and learn to leverage this powerful tool to enhance your productivity and achieve outstanding results.

The key to mastering ChatGPT lies in the way you interact with it. Throughout this book, you'll embark on a journey to unlock the secrets of advanced prompting techniques and a novel approach to composing them, uncovering the hidden depths of ChatGPT's capabilities.

Prepare to separate yourself from casual users and become a ChatGPT prompting expert, bending the technology to your will and extracting optimal value and insights that others can only dream of. The power to harness this groundbreaking technology is within your grasp.

Turn to the next chapter, and let your path to mastery begin.

CHAPTER 1
ESSENTIALS YOU NEED TO KNOW TO BECOME A PROMPTING MASTER

"The limits of my language mean the limits of my world."
— *Ludwig Wittgenstein*

"In the end, it was all about the conversation." Such are the words of many a successful, or failed, relationship. One's way with words is like a sum of the many moving parts of a language that build on each other to bring about the magic and chemistry or lack thereof of interactions, whether these are relationships, magic spells, or power.

Today, conversations with artificial intelligence like ChatGPT are the key to unlocking magical outcomes, so knowing them is the all-important skill that makes all the difference.

Beginning your journey to unraveling the secrets behind ChatGPT's remarkable capabilities and exploring the techniques to elevate you from a casual user to a prompting master is what this chapter is about. Along this transformative path, you'll delve into the evolution of language models, the inner workings of ChatGPT, and the philosophy behind crafting effective prompts that unlocks its full potential.

Swinging Right Out of the Gate: Examples!

Let's cut to the chase and get right to the point, demonstrating the importance of proper prompting through clear examples before delving into the philosophical and substantive content of the book.

We'll cover prompt engineering techniques in detail in Chapter 3, *"Prompt Engineering Techniques: From Basics to Advanced,"* but for now let's get you started immediately so you'll see the significant impact and just how much a difference attention to prompting makes, using the examples that follow as the staging point for your journey to mastery.

Brevity with Weight: The Inverted Pyramid Technique

In journalism, the most important information should come first such as the Who, What, When, Where, and How so that even if the reader doesn't read beyond the first few paragraphs, they'll have gotten the gist of the story.

In prompting, a similar approach is ideal, albeit for different reasons, and such a seemingly pedestrian yet highly effective prompting method is the "inverted pyramid" technique. This approach, like in journalism, structures the prompt in a way that places the most important and attention-grabbing information first, followed by progressively less critical details.

It's very simple so is often ignored, but is a useful strategy that helps to capture the AI's attention and encourages it to provide the most relevant response:

1. Start with the most crucial piece of information or the main question, stated in clear terms
2. Provide essential supporting details and context
3. Add supplemental or background information as necessary

Example 1:

- Without inverted pyramid: *"What are some healthy meals I can prepare for my family? We prefer plant-based dishes, and my daughter has a gluten intolerance."*
- With inverted pyramid: *"Suggest gluten-free, plant-based meal ideas for my family."*

Example 2:

- Without inverted pyramid: *"I'm planning a trip to Italy in the summer and want to know the must-visit destinations, taking into account that I enjoy art, history, and local cuisine."*
- With inverted pyramid: *"Recommend must-visit Italian destinations for an art, history, and cuisine enthusiast."*

The Inverted Pyramid is but one example of various outstanding methods for generating optimal results. There's more.

Creativity-focused techniques:

Constraint-Driven Prompts: Introduce specific limitations to your prompt, like making it answer in a specific form, to encourage creativity, to constrain the results to a range, or to simply challenge the model.

Example: "Describe the beauty of a sunset in a haiku."

Example: "Summarize the transcript of our Zoom meeting in the style of a Shakespearean play."

Forced Associations: Combine unrelated concepts, challenging ChatGPT to find connections, no matter how loosely, and make it think creatively.

Example: "How can the principles of minimalism be applied to improve time management?"

Creative Rephrasing: Use unconventional restatements of concepts to encourage ChatGPT to think creatively and generate imaginative, even novel responses.

Example: "If colors had personalities, how would you describe the character of the color blue?"

Anticipating Unique Outcomes through Guided Storytelling: Describe a context or scenario, or rephrase a concept, in an unconventional way to see what possible outcomes ChatGPT may come up with that you may not have thought about.

Example: "Begin a story about a young detective solving a mystery in a small town. Introduce a surprising twist halfway through the story."

The Analogy Technique: Ask ChatGPT to explain a concept or situation through an analogy, encouraging it to pull out the stops for its creativity or to consider potential concepts creatively.

Example: "Explain the process of photosynthesis using an analogy involving a factory."

Perspective-focused techniques:

Roleplay Prompts: One of the more common yet powerful techniques for effective prompting, in this technique you assign roles or personas to ChatGPT, encouraging it to provide a deeper answer from the function, perspective, and point of view of the assigned persona.

Example: "Imagine you are a renowned chef. How would you describe the art of cooking?"

Example: "You are an expert copywriter specializing in B2B. List potentially high-converting headlines for a social media ad campaign for a contract manufacturer."

The *"In the Shoes of"* Technique: Let ChatGPT walk in the shoes of an expert operator in the field of the target subject and assume the perspective of such an expert, the identity of a historical figure, or an embodiment of a fictional character, to generate unique insights.

> *Example: "Imagine you are Albert Einstein. How would you explain the theory of relativity in simple terms?"*

The Expert Panel: Make ChatGPT provide opinions or explanations from the perspectives of different experts in a specific field.

> *Example: "How would an economist, a psychologist, and a biologist explain the concept of happiness?"*

Critical thinking and problem-solving techniques:

Socratic Questioning and Laddering Technique: Use a series of strategic questions to guide ChatGPT toward a specific conclusion, a deeper understanding, or a comprehensive exploration of a topic.

> *Example: "What are the primary colors? How do they combine to create secondary colors? What happens when all primary colors are mixed?"*

The Debate Technique: This is among the most fun, yet insightful techniques used to great effect. Present two opposing viewpoints and ask ChatGPT to provide arguments for both sides.

> *Example: "Discuss the advantages and disadvantages of renewable energy sources versus fossil fuels."*

Contrasting Viewpoints Technique: Related to the Debate Technique above, in this technique, you ask ChatGPT to make a counterargument or counterexample to a given concept to enable you to see the perspective of the other side.

> *Example: Topic: Should college education be free for everyone?*

> *Prompt: "Make a counterargument for why college education should not be free for everyone."*

Multi-Step Problem Solving: Encouraging ChatGPT to think critically and demonstrate problem-solving skills by presenting a complex problem that requires several steps to solve.

Example: "How can a company reduce its carbon footprint and become more environmentally friendly while maintaining profitability?"

Techniques that promote deeper exploration:

Laddering Technique: Start with a broad question and narrow the focus down through follow-up questions, encouraging a more comprehensive approach toward the understanding of a topic.

Example: "What is machine learning? How is it applied in natural language processing? Can you provide an example?"

***"What If"* Scenarios and Hypothetical Situations:** Propose hypothetical situations to explore alternative perspectives, unique viewpoints, or potential consequences.

Example: "What if the internet was never invented? How would that affect modern society?"

The Chain Prompt: Channel your inner inquisitive badgering child and create a sequence of related prompts that build on each other, encouraging the deeper exploration of a topic while focused on the subject at large.

Example: "What is the greenhouse effect? How does it impact global temperatures? What are the consequences of rising global temperatures?"

Techniques that challenge the AI's capabilities:

Reverse-Engineering Answers: This is another one of the most fun and useful techniques. Instead of asking a question, provide the answer first, then implicitly or explicitly challenge ChatGPT to generate relevant questions or problems. That is, instead of providing a statement and asking for an explanation, instead, give the explanation and request the original statement.

Example: "The answer is 'photosynthesis.' What is the question?"

Example: "What statement would lead to this explanation: 'It's a law in physics that states that energy cannot be created or destroyed, only converted from one form to another.'?"

Role Reversal: Ask ChatGPT to pose questions to you about a specific topic, helping you to think critically and gain new insights.

Example: "As an AI interested in learning about climate change, what questions should I ask you?"

Anatomy of a Good Prompt

The Simple and Straightforward Formula

The basic form of a prompt is like what people would normally use a search engine for, asking a question.

Example: "What is the capital of the UK?"

This is straightforward and there is no need to add anything more.

In other, if not most cases, you will need to either make follow-up prompts to query the AI further, or add context to your query, or prompt. Context in this case means any additional information, data, instructions, conditions, descriptions, attributes, etc. that would be useful for the model to know in processing and performing your prompt.

While there may be a million ways to skin the cat that is ChatGPT, there are a few key components that comprise the anatomy of a good prompt to ensure clarity, quality, and effectiveness in answers.

While each prompt is different and you must adjust as well as adapt your prompt composition accordingly, a good generic format to serve as your base consists of six parts.

1. Purpose

Define the "why," primary goal, or objective of the prompt, as well as clearly state the intent, such as whether you are gathering information, seeking advice, generating content, or exploring creative ideas.

2. Role, Context and Background Information

Set the scene. Tell ChatGPT the role (e.g. expert, doctor, etc.) it will play in taking your prompt, plus your situation by providing relevant background information, stating what you are trying to accomplish, or other contextual clues as well as specifics like the role you want it to play. This seemingly innocuous polish goes a long way toward helping it generate more accurate, relevant responses.

3. Topic

Make a clear and concise statement of the subject matter that the prompt is addressing.

4. Instruction and Task: Specificity and Precision Rule

This is the meat of your prompt, if you will. As such, it is important to always remember to be precise in your request, and to help narrow down the scope of the response to ensure that the output aligns with your expectations. Give your directive, and tell it what you want it to do in the clearest terms possible. Where applicable, specify the desired format, ideal process, length, and other expectations you may have for the response.

In fact, specify the *constraints* you'd like to place on the results. While specifying constraints is an important enough topic to warrant its own component in this anatomy, it is integrated here to maximize the flow of this all-important part of the prompt.

5. Tone and Outcome Desired

Instead of just awaiting a generic response, indicate the tone or style in which you'd like the answer to be formed because it makes a difference in the way the generated text matches the appropriate voice or mood. Point out if you'd like the result to be formal, for example, or casual, humorous, or informative.

6. Provide Examples and Clarify

This is an optional step, but depending on the context can help make for accurate and meaningful results. Include examples or sample responses to the prompt to clarify your expectations and help guide as well as hammer home to ChatGPT what you're trying to do.

As needed, you can also disambiguate to ensure everything is clear, making sure there are no two ways of understanding what you're trying to convey, effectively plugging any holes to its complete and utter understanding.

Note that these components *do not* need to all be in place, in sequence, or follow the exact format; nor do they need to be complete and explicitly exist in every prompt. Adjust accordingly, and keep, add, or remove as necessary, remembering only to be as clear and precise as possible about what you want, and using the context and your better judgment to complete the prompt composition.

After-Prompt Actions

The six components above are meant to comprise the generic format of a good prompt. Once you've executed it, you can additionally consider the tips below as additional steps you can take to refine and squeeze more potential value from it.

7. Open-endedness and Prompt Type

Encourage creativity and exploration by crafting open-ended questions or scenarios. This allows ChatGPT to think beyond standard responses and provide more imaginative and engaging answers. Consider different prompt types, such as open-ended, closed-ended, or multiple-choice questions, to achieve the desired outcome.

8. Refine: Follow-up Questions

While components 1 to 6 are usually part of a single prompt, this part, Refinement, is meant to be made after ChatGPT provides a response but you find that it hasn't completely satisfied your expectations, or if a clarification opportunity presents itself.

This phase can be used to follow up on ChatGPT's response and continue the conversation, encouraging deeper exploration and understanding. You proceed and run the prompt again, repeating the activity as you undergo the process of clarification until every point has been conveyed.

Basic Examples: Putting the Components to Work

Example 1:

- *Purpose:* Gather information about a historical event
- *Context:* The context is doing research for a historical event that took place in the 20th century that will be part of a novel being written.
- *Topic:* The Cuban Missile Crisis
- *Specificity:* Explain the main causes and consequences of the Cuban Missile Crisis.
- *Tone:* Informative
- *Provide examples:* Include examples of key events and decisions made during the crisis.

Prompt: "I'm doing research for a novel I'm writing that is set in Cuba during the time of Kennedy. Explain the main causes and consequences of the Cuban Missile Crisis, a significant historical event that took place in the 20th century. Include examples of key events and decisions made during the crisis, and use an informative tone."

Example 2:

- *Purpose:* Seek advice on how to improve public speaking skills
- *Context:* The context is self-improvement in the domain of public speaking.
- *Topic:* Tips for better public speaking
- *Specificity:* List five practical tips to improve public speaking skills.
- *Tone:* Supportive
- *Provide examples:* Include examples/anecdotes that illustrate the effectiveness of each tip.

Prompt: "I am trying to begin the process of self-improvement and need good advice to maximize this endeavor. Please list five practical tips that can help someone improve their public speaking skills. Provide anecdotes that illustrate the effectiveness of each tip, and use a supportive tone."

Example 3:

- *Purpose:* Generate a creative short story
- *Context:* The context is a fictional story set in a magical forest.
- *Topic:* A magical forest adventure
- *Specificity:* Write a short story of approximately 300 words about an adventure in a magical forest.
- *Tone:* Engaging
- *Provide examples:* Incorporate vivid descriptions and examples of the magical elements encountered in the forest.

Prompt: "Craft an engaging short story of around 300 words about an adventure in a magical forest. Incorporate vivid descriptions and samples of the magical elements encountered in the forest."

Example 4:

- *Purpose:* Improve time management skills

- *Context:* The context is a busy work environment with multiple tasks and deadlines.
- *Topic:* Effective time management strategies
- *Specificity:* List five time management strategies that can be applied in a busy work environment to improve productivity.
- *Tone:* Informative
- *Provide examples:* Include real-life examples or scenarios for each strategy to demonstrate its effectiveness.

Prompt: "In an informative tone, list five time management strategies that can be applied in a busy work environment to improve productivity. Include real-life scenarios for each strategy to demonstrate its effectiveness."

Example 5:

- *Purpose:* Encourage team collaboration
- *Context:* The context is a group project in a professional setting.
- *Topic:* Techniques to enhance team collaboration
- *Specificity:* Describe three techniques that can be used to enhance team collaboration in a group project, focusing on communication and cooperation.
- *Tone:* Persuasive
- *Provide examples:* Provide examples of successful team collaborations that employed these techniques.

Prompt: "In a persuasive tone, describe three techniques that can be used to enhance team collaboration in a group project, focusing on communication and cooperation. Provide cases of successful team collaborations that employed these techniques."

Example 6:

- *Purpose:* Optimize workplace organization
- *Context:* The context is a cluttered office space that hinders productivity.

- *Topic:* Organizational methods to improve efficiency
- *Specificity:* Suggest three organizational methods to declutter and optimize an office space for increased efficiency.
- *Tone:* Actionable
- *Provide examples:* Share practical tips or examples of how implementing these methods can lead to a more efficient work environment.

Prompt: "Suggest three organizational methods to declutter and optimize an office space for increased efficiency. Share practical tips [note: examples] of how implementing these methods can lead to a more efficient work environment. Use an actionable tone."

Example 7:

- *Purpose:* Explore a philosophical concept
- *Context:* The context is the philosophical idea of existentialism.
- *Topic:* Existentialism and personal freedom
- *Specificity:* Discuss the relationship between existentialism and personal freedom, addressing the concept's key principles.
- *Tone:* Analytical
- *Provide examples:* Use examples from the works of prominent existentialist philosophers to support your discussion.

Prompt: "Discuss the relationship between existentialism and personal freedom, addressing the concept's key principles. Use instances from the works of prominent existentialist philosophers to support your discussion. Use an analytical tone."

Example 8:

- *Purpose:* Obtain a recipe for a delicious dessert
- *Context:* The context is a dessert that features chocolate as the main ingredient.
- *Topic:* Chocolate soufflé recipe

- *Specificity:* Provide a detailed recipe for a chocolate soufflé, including ingredients and step-by-step instructions.
- *Tone:* Clear and concise
- *Provide examples:* Include any helpful tips or variations to the recipe, as well as presentation suggestions.

Prompt: "In a clear and concise manner, provide a detailed recipe for a chocolate soufflé, including ingredients and step-by-step instructions. Include any helpful tips or variations to the recipe, as well as presentation suggestions."

Example 9:

- *Purpose:* Explore future technology
- *Context:* The context is a world 50 years from now, with advancements in technology beyond our current imagination.
- *Topic:* Futuristic transportation systems
- *Specificity:* Describe two innovative transportation systems that could revolutionize the way people travel 50 years from now.
- *Tone:* Imaginative
- *Provide examples:* Explain how these transportation systems would function and what their impact would be on society.

Prompt: "Describe two innovative transportation systems that could revolutionize the way people travel 50 years from now. Explain how these transportation systems would function and what their impact would be on society. Use an imaginative, creative style."

Example 10:

- *Purpose:* Encourage environmental awareness
- *Context:* The context is the current global climate crisis and the need for immediate action to preserve our planet.
- *Topic:* Small lifestyle changes to reduce carbon footprint

- *Specificity:* Identify three small lifestyle changes that individuals can make to reduce their carbon footprint and contribute to a more sustainable future.
- *Tone:* Motivational
- *Provide examples:* Explain the benefits of each change and provide examples of the positive impact they could have on the environment.

Prompt: "In a motivational tone, identify three small lifestyle changes that individuals can make to reduce their carbon footprint and contribute to a more sustainable future. Explain the benefits of each change and provide examples of the positive impact they could have on the environment."

These varied examples showcase the flexibility of the prompt components, demonstrating how they can be applied to a wide range of topics and genres.

To think, these don't even include things like assuming roles, concepts like reverse engineering, or applying techniques that are yet forthcoming. They barely scratch the surface, and in succeeding chapters, you'll learn to use and add components to these basic examples to really make your prompts pop.

Ready, Fire, Aim

Having seen the examples first, now we can return to the grounding and environment surrounding ChatGPT, now that you're aware that calibrating your mind to creative and clear prompt formation provides results that are different like night and day compared to the results derived from the usual suboptimal ways.

As such, it's time to peer behind the curtains of ChatGPT and its mothership that is OpenAI to get a broad sense of how we got here, and use the appreciation from knowing that background to better whisper the kind of knowledge to the machine that invokes your desired outcomes.

All Learning Begins with a "Spark"

Expertise starts with the spark of curiosity or a desire to learn, that when applied, ignites combustion that propels your mastery forward.

The way to such mastery for ChatGPT isn't made by memorizing strings of text or a recipe book you have to constantly refer to. It's done through applying the knowledge of principles and theory behind the concept and technology. Only then will you have the real command of ChatGPT. So let's begin with its backstory.

The Evolution of Language Models

ChatGPT's "overnight" success actually took many years. Its explosive popularity surprised even its own creators, to the collective dismay of its competitors, because when it was unleashed into the world at the end of November, 2022, its underlying technology— GPT-3 at the time— was already being privately used by many in research and industry and didn't seem to cause a ruckus.

But this all changed when OpenAI wrapped a user-friendly interface to their AI that things really went crazy, hitting 1 million users in its first 5 days, and 100 million users in two months, making it the fastest-growing app in history.

ChatGPT is built on a *large language model* (LLM), a product of a new generation of "generative AI" algorithms that can be used to create increasingly convincing new content like text, images, video, audio, and even synthetic data.

LLMs represent a type of deep learning architecture called Transformers, the predominant type of deep learning model made of a neural network that gains an understanding of context and meanings by excelling at analyzing relationships between sequential input data, such as those used in prompts.

These consist of many parameters— also called weights that are essentially variables— in the model that can be used to infer new content— trained on huge quantities of data, using self-supervised learning, which was a paradigm shift from the previous ways of training specialized supervised models for specific tasks.

The concept of GPT itself was built on the modern Transformer model that was introduced in a groundbreaking paper by a team at Google in 2017, itself building on other technologies and concepts before that.

Advances in AI language models have been rapidly increasing over the years. Early statistical language models relied on what are now seemingly primitive methods like word frequency and occurrence to predict words and phrases made them struggle with complex linguistic structures and downright wouldn't understand the context.

But the evolution of language models continued its inexorable march, paving the way for the next stage, which was the emergence of deep learning techniques that included recurrent neural networks (RNNs) and long short-term memory (LSTM) networks that captured context better and, to a limited degree, remember and process past inputs by maintaining an internal state. These technologies still suffered from eating a lot of computational resources and myriad challenges in handling long-range dependencies.

This changed with the breakthrough in 2017 of the development of the Transformer architecture that introduced the concept of self- attention mechanisms (the original paper in 2017 from the team at Google was titled *"Attention is All You Need"*).

Transformers, after all, are language models, trained on large amounts of raw text in a self-supervised way in a type of training from which the objective is computed from the inputs of the model in a way that reinforces itself without needing humans to label the data or intervene.

Transformers adopt the mechanism of "self-attention," which allows the model to attend to different parts of an input sequence (input data such as parts of a prompt), assigning different weights to the significance of each part, while "attention" allows the model to attend to different parts of another sequence.

This effectively enhances some parts of the input while diminishing the other parts, enabling the network to devote more focus to the smaller, more important parts of the data by computing a representation of the different positions and enabling the model to "understand" the context and overall input so it can process and produce superior results.

Divining which part of the data is more important than the other depends on various elements such as context as well as the makeup of the algorithm itself.

These mechanisms allowed the models to efficiently process long sequences of text, and capture context more effectively without the need for forcing a sequential processing structure.

OpenAI's GPT series, which includes ChatGPT, is built upon such a Transformer architecture, resulting in the advanced capabilities we see today that only seem to advance and compound in its abilities more rapidly as time passes. The simple mechanism of trying to predict what words will follow a given input has gone a very long way.

In the next section, we'll explore the Transformer architecture and its impact on *natural language processing* (NLP), as well as how it has shaped the way we engage with AI-powered language models.

Understanding ChatGPT's Architecture

In this section, we'll take a peek under the hood of ChatGPT and examine its architecture, breaking down its building blocks to uncover the secrets behind its ability to generate complex, coherent responses which is what got the world in a tailspin.

The Evolution of NLP Models: From RNNs and LSTMs to Transformer Architecture

Before the Transformer architecture, natural language processing (NLP) systems depended heavily on *Recurrent Neural Networks* (RNNs) and *Long Short-Term Memory* (LSTM) networks, which we covered briefly in the section above.

RNNs process input data sequentially, making them suitable for tasks involving text, even though they process text one word at a time and therefore tend to be slow and inefficient. LSTMs are a type of RNN that were developed to overcome these inefficiencies by capturing longer-range dependencies and succeeding for the most part... except that it still processed text sequentially, eventually becoming its own can of worms that needed fixing.

When the Google team introduced the Transformer architecture, effectively revolutionizing NLP, it replaced RNNs and LSTMs with self-attention mechanisms as we learned in the previous section, enabling models to process text in parallel rather than sequentially, a seemingly innocuous shift but which would later result in orders of magnitude of change. An innovation that reduced training times significantly— always a plus in this game— but more importantly, it enhanced the model's ability to capture long-range dependencies.

This means it more accurately understands the relationship between words—even those far apart from each other— in a sentence or text phrase; a limitation plaguing older RNNs and LSTMs, making the Transformer architecture a game-changer that transformed the field of NLP, and paved the way for a new era of language processing, and AI adoption.

An Example

Consider the sentence, *"My dog, which is sitting on the mat, suddenly yelped and scrambled out of the room."* Here, the words "dog" and "scrambled" are far apart, yet have a dependency on each other because the subject of the sentence is the dog, and the action is the scrambling.

Previously, with RNNs and LSTMs for example, capturing this long-range dependency was hard, and resulted in inaccurate or incorrect responses. (This is different from the concept of "hallucinations" in Transformer models, which we will cover later.) But the Transformer's "self-attention" mechanisms captured such long- range dependencies, allowing it to better "understand" the sentence, thereby orienting its responses to the correct, accurate, and coherent responses.

Aftermath

This change was like a tectonic shift that would reverberate not just in the field but across time and around the world, effectively culminating in a place in history where we could point and say, "*This*. This is when it happened," when the world woke up to AI that was available– an AI people used to say was constantly 30 years away– here, now.

Its seeming science-fiction allure was turning less and less fictional by the day. The entire tech sector would jump all over it and create a tidal wave of development and adoption the likes of which we've never seen before, comparable only to the most fundamental of changes like computing, the Internet, and mobile phones.

The GPT Series and OpenAI

Capitalizing on the Transformer architecture, OpenAI, which was already experimenting with various AI pursuits including game AIs that beat the best human players in complex network strategy games such as the multiplayer online battle arena phenomenon *DotA*, then developed the Generative Pre-trained Transformer (GPT) series, which evolved through multiple iterations, fits and starts, but that generally made unstoppable progress in terms of model size, complexity, capabilities and more.

There were many reasons to attribute to this such as having a good pedigree, an incredibly talented team, a storied history, and most of all, in the case of the GPT series, a concept— the Transformer architecture— that simply worked.

The first iteration that laid the foundation for the series, GPT, seemed to be severely limited compared to its successors, in terms of performance, model size, and training data, but became a landmark because of one successful quality: it demonstrated the potential of the Transformer architecture in natural language processing tasks, and it worked.

Then OpenAI just moved from strength to strength from there.

GPT-2 marked a substantial leap in language model capabilities and parameter size (jumping from mere millions to 1.5 billion parameters) that resulted not just in an incremental improvement on the original GPT, but especially in a remarkable ability to generate coherent and contextually relevant responses.

It almost seems quaint by the standards a mere few years later, but at the time it was so good it sparked discussions on AI ethical implications for its power that OpenAI initially withheld the full model from public access. A pattern not lost in later generations.

GPT-3 made more orders of magnitude improvement over the last generation that on the outset, it seems like you're just throwing billions of parameters willy-nilly when in fact, each bit of these actually mattered, with the company making it clear that their focus was improving on the algorithm and technology instead of just dumping more and more data to the thing.

In this, GPT-3 demonstrated an impressive understanding of context and language structure, enabling it to perform a wide range of tasks, not the least of which was to impress the hell out of people in the way it intelligently engaged with them. Just as importantly, GPT-3 actualized the capacity to perform a wide range of tasks that included content generation, translation, and summarization, which opened up real new possibilities and applications for AI technology that not so long ago were clumped in the "not possible" or "30 years away" file.

ChatGPT built on the success of GPT-3 with a rich set of additions and capabilities, but that was essentially a user-friendly– if overtly simple– interface, designed to facilitate interactive, dynamic, and engaging conversations. But it exceeded this by including refinements that produced natural, engaging, and context-aware dialogues. It also integrated the specialized capabilities of OpenAI's specialized models (such as the *Codex* model for coding, among others) all neatly made part of a happy little package, making it a powerful tool for a wide array of applications, whether for personal use and everyday life, to work, business, education, and various professional fields.

The arrival of GPT-4 only cemented OpenAI's leadership role because of the power intrinsic to the model, but also the breadth of extensibility, potential, and flexibility that included a flavor of it getting integrated into Microsoft's Bing, and became an industry and historic "iPhone Moment" type of shift that secured its place in the hearts, attention, and life of developers everywhere; securing a rapidly growing ecosystem, sub-industry, and explosion of products and services with wildly different use-cases but that mostly act like powerful wrappers and extensions to the base GPT model.

Competitors were caught flat-footed, scurried (and failed) to catch up, while OpenAI suddenly became the incumbent in a field so vast that it will encompass everything we do in life. So much so that the fears, risks, and implications of AI– both good and bad– that used to exist but were usually closer to the backwaters of the general public, suddenly got thrust into the spotlight because of its sudden staggering popularity and the clarity with which ChatGPT's technology, and AI in general, is finally proven to work as advertised.

Fine-Tuning and Datasets

To ensure that ChatGPT has a strong foundation in language understanding while also being adaptable for specialized applications, it is trained through a two-step process that includes *pre-training* on a massive dataset, and *fine-tuning* using custom or smaller task-specific datasets tailored for specific tasks.

In fact, the latter process is something many specialized applications that use the OpenAI or ChatGPT APIs so to train the model(s) to their product, product set, or company's datasets and enable it to knowledgeably interact with users regarding specific points about the company and its products or services that normally wouldn't be available in a general way, and allows the model to provide more relevant and accurate responses that are tailored to the specific needs of the application and its users.

Pre-training

During the pre-training phase, vast amounts of data taken from a huge array of sources from— but not limited to— around the Internet become the sources that ChatGPT is fed from which it learns to understand language patterns and structures. The process allows the model to develop a broad understanding of language, context, and knowledge in different domains while setting the stage for the other step of the process, and taking great strides to ensure the datasets being used are high-quality, diverse, (ideally) ethically sourced, and cleaned.

After all, you wouldn't want to have a whiz-bang of a product only to be in the crosshairs of lawsuits and scandals down the road, especially when bait-hungry media will pounce on anything to get eyeballs and clicks.

These sources vary and are numerous, including such esteemed institutions like Wikipedia ('natch), web-crawl data sets maintained by CommonCrawl and OpenAI's own OpenWebText, BooksCorpus, and even... well, Reddit.

One can argue about the many subreddits being such entertaining cesspools but there is no arguing about the value of dialogue that is exchanged on there going beyond the mere zeitgeist of the modern world, even though the job of cleaning that particular provenance of data might not be one we'd exactly envy.

Fine-tuning

To adapt the model with specific tasks in various domains, and improving its performance, ChatGPT undergoes fine-tuning with smaller, specialized, and curated datasets.

This phase involves training the model on carefully selected data that are often generated with the help of human reviewers (who of course follow OpenAI guidelines).

These are smaller datasets that are specific to certain tasks. Think of it like giving ChatGPT a personalized lesson to learn how to handle a specific job. Or like a tutor who specializes in the specific topic you want to learn.

OpenAI uses this process to add to the general breadth of the corpus used in its models, while companies utilizing a GPT model or one based on ChatGPT might use this process to train the AI for answering customer support questions, for example.

During the fine-tuning process, ChatGPT's "knowledge" is adjusted to better suit the specialized task. This is done by providing it with examples of what you want it to learn and adjusting the weights in the neural network that makes up the AI.

This can involve a surprisingly simple text-based process that requires an inordinate amount of care to ensure ChatGPT stays on track, but builds on its existing knowledge and pre-training.

This makes it ready to help you or your users answer questions or perform other tasks related to the topic, like having a very smart assistant who knows a lot— even veritably perform like an expert—

about a particular subject, while also being ready and knowledgeable about any germane topic, ready to help you out, serving its function as a versatile, valuable, and capable tool that can tackle a wide range of activities, such as from casual conversations to professional tasks.

A Meta-tool

The output of this process is a versatile model that charms multitudes while becoming a valuable tool— and to more and more each day, an indispensable one—that can effectively handle specialized tasks that deliver relevant, contextually appropriate responses that are mostly accurate, and used right, strikingly useful. I say "mostly" because there are known cases of inaccuracies, commonly known as *hallucinations*, and it spews it in such style and aplomb that you can hardly doubt it.

But still, when you combine the power of the Transformer architecture with the advances of the GPT series, and then throw that into a meticulous training process, you hit all the notes to go gangbusters on a symphonic masterpiece that shocks and inspires awe. And that's exactly what happened.

How ChatGPT Generates Responses

Gaining mastery over a subject isn't just about knowing the mechanics of how to use it, but knowing what makes it tick. To be an AI Whisperer for ChatGPT, you can better appreciate its capabilities once you understand the process behind its response generation. Thankfully, you don't have to count to infinity to learn this, as I've got simplified explanations for you, so you'll know how ChatGPT generates responses, from tokenization to selecting words and phrases to process.

Tokenization and Preprocessing

ChatGPT processes text by breaking it down into tokens, the smallest units of text that the model can understand, where the input text is split into words, subwords, or characters, depending on the language and model architecture. Such "preprocessing" and "tokenization" also involve sanitizing the text, handling special characters, and converting the tokens into a format that the model can then process. We'll delve deeper into this topic in Chapter 2.

The Transformer Architecture

You've met the Transformer architecture in the sections above (specifically 1.2), and it sits at the core of ChatGPT, consisting of self-attention mechanisms and feed-forward neural networks as described there. The Transformer processes input tokens in parallel rather than sequentially as was the case of older models of RNNs and LSTMs, which enabled efficient handling of long sequences among its many talents, helping it understand the context and relationships between tokens, which are in turn crucial for generating coherent responses.

Decoding and Output Generation

After ChatGPT processes the tokens from the input sequence (such as from prompts), it generates an output sequence in turn by choosing words and phrases that maximize the probability of a coherent response based on the magnitude of assets used to train it.

There are various techniques used in the decoding process that may just put you to sleep if we had to go into detail about them here (a couple of them are called "beam search" or "nucleus sampling" in case you needed something fancy to say at a party), so it's not necessary for our purposes. But what's important is that the process undergoes this decoding step which balances the tradeoff between creativity and consistency, before the generated tokens are then converted back into human-readable, human-understandable text that forms the response you receive. This process and its nuances produce high-quality responses. And we'll discuss this further alongside the practical aspects of mastery as we progress through the book.

The Importance of Effective Prompts

While merely saying "open sesame" in a prompt will open the door somewhat, knowing how to craft prompts effectively is essential for guiding ChatGPT to produce the desired output. And mastering this art of prompt engineering enables you to significantly enhance ChatGPT's output, opening its doors wide to reveal the wealth of secrets that lie within.

We'll cover the details in Chapter 3, but consider the following guidelines as part of your prompting philosophy:

- Be clear and concise. But don't be lacking, either. Don't waste words in an effort to be descriptive but come out as ambiguous instead. Keep your prompts straightforward and to the point, without neglecting to include all the necessary details as well.
- Specify the desired format. State the required format you expect of the answer clearly, guiding ChatGPT towards the expected output instead of blindly hitting return and hoping for the best.
- Anticipate potential misunderstandings. This happens a lot so it's worth expanding on. What may seem clear to you can be ambiguous or downright confusing to someone else. ChatGPT is no different because it can't read your mind (yet) and will try to uncover your intent if you ask a question or do a test that can have different meanings. Thus, identify potential ambiguities in your question beforehand and address them in your prompt, preemptively tackling any confusion. If you asked this question of your cousin's friend's girlfriend's mother's uncle's grandma for example, would it clearly understand your question and intent?
- Use context. Set the stage and supply ChatGPT with relevant background information about your inquiry to help it better grasp what you're asking.

- Use examples. Believe it or not, ChatGPT actually carefully considers examples you provide in its attempt to understand your question, and combines these with the rest of your input to arrive at an accurate assessment of what you want and help it get better equipped with an accurate response.
- Set the tone. Indicate the style, format, or nuance you want the AI to adopt in its response, so it hits your expectations and saves you the trouble of interpreting it for your purposes when it would gladly do it for you without batting an eye.
- Try to be precise with your expected results. If you want a bulleted-list summary of the minutes of your meeting, a markdown table containing a distillation of review criteria, a sanitized version of a controversial script, a long defense of the opposing side to better prepare for a debate or a host of other output, cite what you expect will be the shape of your expected results and it will better comply when it doesn't have to second- guess what you desire.

Factors Affecting Prompt Quality

Several factors contribute to the effectiveness of a prompt, such as clarity, context, specificity, and the use of constraints. Mastering these elements allows you to create prompts that yield more accurate and relevant responses, ensuring that your interaction with ChatGPT is efficient and productive.

- *Clarity:* Make sure your prompt is easily understood and free from ambiguity.
- *Context:* Provide ample background information to help the AI comprehend the scope of your inquiry.
- *Specificity:* Be precise in your request, steering the AI towards the desired response.
- *Constraints:* Impose limitations or boundaries when necessary to keep the AI focused on the task at hand.

- *Tone and style:* Tailor the tone and style of your prompt to match the desired response, whether formal, casual, or creative.
- *Iterative refinement:* Utilize the AI's previous responses to refine your prompts and guide it toward more accurate answers. Something even more profound than it sounds.

Exploring Different Prompting Techniques

There is no universal approach to prompting, while there are timeless principles that mixed together provide for what is like an infinite array of possibilities.

Experimenting with various techniques, such as iterative prompting, incremental questioning, and altering the tone or style of your prompts, can help you discover the most effective methods for your specific use case.

In this way, understanding and adapting these techniques will allow you to be better equipped to take command and extract your valuable, intended answers from ChatGPT.

We'll devote more details to this in Chapter 3, but in the spirit of getting you a taste of what it's all about immediately, here's a broad overview of the possibilities.

- *Iterative prompting:* Hone your prompts through multiple iterations, adjusting them based on the AI's previous responses.
- *Incremental questioning:* Decompose complex questions into smaller, more manageable queries, guiding the AI through the topic step-by-step.
- *Tone and style variation:* Modify the tone, style, or formality of your prompts to elicit diverse types of responses.
- *Inverted questioning:* Ask the AI to generate questions related to your topic, helping you gain deeper insights into the subject.
- *Leveraging constraints:* Introduce specific constraints, such as word limits or content restrictions, to direct the AI's output.

- *Comparisons and analogies:* Employ comparisons or analogies in your prompts to assist ChatGPT in understanding the context and generating more insightful responses.

Strengths and Limitations of ChatGPT

No AI is perfect, and ChatGPT has its own balance of strengths and limitations. In this section, we will discuss the areas where ChatGPT excels and the challenges it faces, which can help you better utilize the model to your advantage, and better coax it to do your bidding.

Strengths

ChatGPT excels in a wide variety of tasks, and that is a big understatement. This includes answering questions, providing recommendations, assisting in projects, and generating creative content. Its ability to comprehend the context and the relationships between (input and) tokens feel out of this world when you first come in contact with it, and this makes it highly effective in producing coherent and relevant responses.

Furthermore, its versatility allows it to adapt to a wide range of topics and domains, making it an invaluable tool for numerous applications and the countless souls who use it regularly, many of whom unknowingly have gotten so accustomed to its multiplier effect on their productivity and lives that they don't even realize their growing dependency to it.

Especially so when others are upping their game and productivity by utilizing it as a tool that at the very least, people have to use it just to keep up, but otherwise realize gains that they can't do without it anymore.

Limitations

Despite its strengths, ChatGPT has its limitations. Among the most widely known is the phenomenon of "hallucinations," where it might generate plausible-sounding but incorrect, or in rare occasions even nonsensical answers. It can also be sensitive to the phrasing of the input prompt, providing different responses based on slight variations. At the same time, it may sometimes be overly verbose or repetitive and may not always ask clarifying questions when faced with ambiguous queries.

This is why the likes of Google and other large companies were reluctant to release their large language models (LLMs) to the wild until OpenAI forced it on them. While ChatGPT (and practically all early LLMs in general) is adept at a multitude of functions and is veritably excellent at them, it is also very effective in convincing users about its expertise in something by the confidence it projects, even if, upon closer examination, it becomes clear it's just been making things up all along.

This is an effect of its primordial function of text prediction and completion, where it works by trying to predict, complete and finish a sentence or task instead of an innate aptitude for thought or awareness. But with the rapid advances in the field, this is improving very rapidly.

And why, if you use it on sensitive or fact-related work, you should take an extra step and constantly verify its results.

Mitigating Limitations

A popular adage in sports and war is how the best defense is a good offense. In prompting, a key to highly effective prompts is the inclusion of a good defense in the form of mitigating a large language model like ChatGPT's known limitations. In fact, sometimes this means exploiting them.

That is, to overcome ChatGPT's limitations and achieve better results to extract more value from the model, it's essential to not just leverage its strengths but also pay attention to its weaknesses. Doing this in a way that does not just try to avoid it, but take advantage of it.

The sooner you recognize and internalize this, the better off you'll be in adapting your interactions with it accordingly.

This includes adjusting your prompts to fit the confines of this awareness, and employing such techniques as noted in earlier sections such as *iterative prompting, incremental questioning,* experimenting with alternative phrasings, providing more context, and setting constraints, among others.

Employing this principle will help you not just navigate the limitations but also subordinate it, then exploit it, on your way to unlocking the full potential of ChatGPT.

Awareness of this paired with putting what you learn into practice more, you'll find how it will not just get easier and start becoming second nature, but also become a growing habit of constant experimentation towards gaining mastery over prompt engineering and constantly improving results.

Overview of the Book

The aim of this book is to provide a comprehensive guide to mastering ChatGPT by enabling you to learn to apply the combination of both the art and the science of its command, delving deep into its inner workings, prompt engineering techniques, practical applications, ethical considerations, and many more.

The book is structured into seven chapters, each designed to progressively enhance your understanding and proficiency in using ChatGPT effectively towards its mastery.

- *Chapter 1:* Essentials You Need To Know To Become A Prompting Master- If you've reached this section by reading the preceding ones, you'll now fully appreciate that this chapter offers a broad overview of ChatGPT and a bird's eye view of its surroundings that include its parent company, its architecture, strengths, limitations, and a wealth of early examples placed even this early in the book to whet your appetite and give you a taste of the joys of knowing the process of proper prompting, as well as a taste of what's to come in succeeding chapters. It also introduces the art of prompting and sets the stage for the rest of the book.

- *Chapter 2: Understanding ChatGPT and AI-Language Models* - This chapter explores in deeper detail the technology and mechanics behind ChatGPT that were touched on in Chapter 1, including ChatGPT's and key concepts of language models such as tokenization, attention mechanisms, and pre-training. It also covers the role of prompting, evals– or evaluation– of AI language model performance, recent advancements in the field of artificial intelligence in general, and the narrower alleys of concern where ChatGPT resides.

- *Chapter 3: Prompt Engineering Techniques: From Basics to Advanced* - This chapter presents the guiding principles of prompt engineering with a range of prompting techniques, and examples. These range from crafting effective questions to utilizing context and managing expectations. From there we'll then explore advanced techniques, which include iterative prompting, dynamic prompting, and controlling response length and format.

- *Chapter 4: Practical Applications of ChatGPT* - Once you know the Who, What, When Where, and Why of ChatGPT and its parent company from previous chapters, you'll appreciate their impact when you see examples of them in action. This chapter is what that is all about, and showcases a wide variety of applications for ChatGPT in areas such as communication, personal projects, entertainment, education, customer service, marketing, product development, and sales optimization.

- *Chapter 5: Ethical Considerations and Responsible AI Usage* - No, this chapter isn't a typical lecture on the merits of ethics and morality, and instead discusses the ethical implications of AI language models like ChatGPT so you can use it to your advantage. In this chapter, we address important issues like bias, manipulation, and privacy, while also exploring topics like AI regulation, guidelines, and content detection techniques that promote responsible usage. This way, you gain an understanding of ethical considerations and turn it into an advantage in tuning, reading, and interpreting the results.

- *Chapter 6: Staying Ahead in the AI Landscape* - Seldom does a technological rising tide capture the imagination of the public so quickly and thoroughly as ChatGPT and this unprecedented ascension in the minds of the public means there is an explosion of activity and advances as a natural consequence. This chapter highlights the importance of staying informed of the rapidly evolving artificial intelligence space by discussing strategies for staying informed about new developments, learning from AI communities, and adapting to the changing world of AI-powered and particularly ChatGPT-enabled applications, enhancements like plugins, and bold new landscapes on the horizon.
- *Chapter 7: Conclusion* - The final chapter wraps up the book, summarizing the key takeaways and emphasizing the importance of continuous learning in the age of AI in general, and the mastery of ChatGPT and prompt engineering in particular.

This book is designed to take you on a journey from understanding the fundamentals of ChatGPT to mastering advanced techniques and exploring practical applications. Along the way, we will address the ethical considerations and challenges posed by AI language models, and equip you with the knowledge and tools to stay ahead in the fast-paced world of AI.

Key takeaways:

- AI language models have evolved from statistical models to the advanced Transformer architecture used in ChatGPT.
- ChatGPT's multifaceted and powerful abilities come from its Transformer architecture, large-scale training, and fine-tuning processes.

- Words matter. ChatGPT is advanced enough to perform really well with what you ask of it, but knowing how to effectively talk to it by way of prompting techniques, is the key to guiding it towards accurate and relevant responses, and your win.
- Understanding ChatGPT's strengths, limitations, and mitigations plays a valuable part in composing effective prompts. On the other hand, ethical considerations are important for responsible AI use, and not getting into trouble down the road.
- Knowing how things are done is very important, but drilling yourself towards expertise is just as essential. That is why experimenting with different prompting techniques to go with putting the techniques you learn from this book will go a long way towards helping you harness ChatGPT to its full potential.

Action steps:

- Reflect on the strengths and limitations of ChatGPT, including steps for mitigating its limitations, and consider how they can impact your use of the model, as well as internalizing these concepts as a philosophy in preparing for prompts you generate.
- Familiarize yourself with the various prompting techniques discussed in this chapter.
- Practice crafting effective prompts using the guidelines provided.

Armed with the broad strokes, in the next chapter, we'll start looking under the hood to see what makes ChatGPT tick and start diving deeper into the world of prompt engineering to transform your interactions with ChatGPT.

CHAPTER 2
UNDERSTANDING CHATGPT AND AI LANGUAGE MODELS

"Language is a process of free creation; its laws and principles are fixed, but the manner in which the principles of generation are used is free and infinitely varied."

— Noam Chomsky

In its pure essence, ChatGPT is the user interface to the normally arcane mechanisms of artificial intelligence, and that simple conduit slapped to the AI is the difference that brought it from relative obscurity outside of the researchers and early adopters, to the global phenomenon it is today. Therefore, in the exciting world of ChatGPT, artificial intelligence meets the art of real human-level conversation, or even better!

We introduced them in Chapter 1; in this chapter we'll revisit them and take a closer look at the technology behind ChatGPT to really up your game by first understanding what makes it tick.

And we'll do it differently. Instead of providing longer explanations or more details to what is essentially a repetition or rehash of the same concepts, we will instead revisit them with clear, simple, and contextual examples.

The technology behind ChatGPT

ChatGPT is like a trusty, super-smart sidekick who is always there to help you out in practically anything you need. This can be something as mundane as writing emails and composing story outlines, to more specialized fields like passing the Bar or medical board exams.

But what makes it really clever is a powerful AI engine known as GPT, which stands for **Generative Pre-trained Transformer**, the seemingly boring name at first glance until you do a double-take and it's actually the coolest name for a technological marvel since Optimus Prime.

It was developed by the fine geniuses at OpenAI and it's like encapsulating the corpus of knowledge of the human race in a virtual box you can poke with your keyboard and mouse through the Internet to do things for you, such as answer questions, write a poem, converse like a chat buddy, or just impress the living daylights out of you.

Think of GPT models like sponges that soak up information from vast amounts of data, starting with text and extending to other modalities like video, audio, and dry dad jokes. For text, they use the concept of *deep learning* to understand and generate human-like text based on the patterns they've learned, which is like having a mini- library in their "brain" that helps them come up with the right words at the right time.

AI Bootcamp: Understanding Self-attention

What sets ChatGPT apart from the rest is the Transformer architecture it's built on. As discussed in Chapter 1, Transformers are like a super-efficient assembly line for language, helping AI models process large-scale language tasks in a snap by using a neat trick called "self-attention" that allows them to focus on different parts of the input text when generating responses, then processing them in a way that makes its outputs more coherent and contextually fitting.

In other words, to put it in the perspective of everyday life, think about how it's super smart like a nerd, without the social awkwardness of a dork (just kidding, but you get the idea).

For a tool that was originally built to predict the next text to what you're typing, it has really come a long way.

With this foundation, now let's talk about key concepts.

Key Concepts: Tokenization, Attention Mechanisms, and Pre-training

The Role of Tokenization in AI language models

Imagine if you had to cut a cake into bite-sized pieces before you could enjoy it, and that's like what the concept of tokenization does for AI language models like ChatGPT, helping the models that ChatGPT uses munch on text to produce amazing results, like a machine that chops down and chomps down its (text) input, breaking the text in a sentence down into smaller pieces called tokens.

For text input processing, these tokens can be words, parts of words, or even single characters, and ChatGPT reads and generates these tokens, making them the building blocks of its understanding.

ChatGPT can also process other modalities like video and audio. In these cases, tokens can be segments of speech or individual sounds for audio, and frames or keyframes for video. These sound segments or video frames are typically used as inputs from which the transcribed or captioned text will be derived and then run through the model.

Different tokenization schemes slice the text differently. For example, some focus on whole words, others on characters, and some on chunks called subwords; with each method having its pros and cons, including speed, efficiency, and the ability to handle rare or unknown words.

Such chopping, slicing, and dicing of such words play a role in affecting the performance of AI models, but ChatGPT can do it like the best of them. So yes, if you ever wondered, it will handle your words any which way you do it, able to handle many languages, if not most of them, while being the most effective in English. But it will still handle your instructions even in Pidgin, Swahili, Esperanto, or Klingon as well as your English without batting an eye.

(And if you ever wondered, yes it will even converse with you in High Valyrian, the fictional language from the Game of Thrones universe; so that even as its grammar and vocabulary are limited to what has been created for the show, it can converse with you in it. *Valar Morghulis!*)

Attention Mechanisms in AI language models

Ever found yourself tuning out during a boring conversation? AI language models like ChatGPT are using a clever trick called *attention mechanisms* to stay focused on the important parts of the text, and they're the secret sauce of these models.

Attention mechanisms help AI language models zero in on the relevant bits of the input prompt (text) like a spotlight shining on the most important words or phrases– that enables the model to capture the relationships between different parts of the text, thereby effectively helping it understand and accordingly making its responses more coherent and contextually appropriate.

Such attention mechanisms are a key feature of the super-efficient language-processing engine that powers ChatGPT, the Transformer architecture.

Pre-training and fine-tuning in AI language models

AI language models like ChatGPT aren't born knowing how to chat; they have to learn through a two-step process called *pre-training* and *fine-tuning*, processes that shape the abilities and, to a lesser but still immensely important degree, the performance of AI models.

ChatGPT learns through this two-step process. First, it goes through "unsupervised pre-training," a kind of crash course in language, if you will. In this way, it is learning from a vast library of text, which is essentially like learning to read by devouring every book in the library, where the model (GPT) picks up and figures out general language patterns and structures by predicting the next word or token in a sequence, the groundwork that lays the foundation for its language understanding.

Fine-tuning, on the other hand, is like ChatGPT's internship, where It gets hands-on experience with a smaller, specific dataset tailored to a particular task or domain, effectively getting trained on specifics, and specific tasks like topics, the birds, and the bees. This helps ChatGPT become more accurate and relevant in those tasks, allowing it to adapt its knowledge to specific situations, making it even more of a conversation whiz and superstar that sashays its way into its users' hearts because combining both steps in its training process is like having a dedicated pal or assistant who is a jack of all trades, but who is also a master of most or all of them (at least, the niche or topics it's been trained on).

This is the big picture about how AI language models learn and adapt, and knowing it gives you the knowledge that helps you to create ever-better prompts and utilize most of ChatGPT's capabilities effectively. Armed with this, let's move to the mechanics of prompting.

The Mechanics of Prompting

Understanding the mechanics of AI language models

Imagine ChatGPT as a masterful storyteller (and you'll soon see why this isn't very far from the truth), one that weaves fantastical tales, but with one main difference from a usual lot of storytellers: the stories it crafts are non-fiction, and they're not the type you enjoy by waiting passively, but instead marvel at how it responds to *your* interaction with it, a story about you, that helps you in whatever you're doing in a way far more than any other normally does.

As impressive as that is, however, peeking behind the curtain to see how it weaves its tales will make you appreciate its talents even more. And exploring the inner workings of AI language models like ChatGPT to reveal the secrets of their storytelling prowess starts with the base function of predicting text.

AI language models learn to tell stories by predicting the next word or token in a sequence, based on the context provided by previous words or tokens of its input (prompt). It's like completing a word puzzle, where the model has to find the perfect fit for each blank space. But unlike a word puzzle that is essentially a game you wouldn't exactly take too seriously to devote a lot of bandwidth to study, AI language models process millions upon billions of these data points.

These models use probability distributions to weigh their options, assigning likelihoods to various scenarios, and different possible continuations, for the given input. It's like placing bets on which word comes next and then picking the most probable option. Instead of relying on luck or intuition, it brings its vast corpus of data and learning to bear in making such a prediction.

Such AI language models generate text by sampling from these probability distributions, creating sentences that flow smoothly and make sense, for you who is prompting it. The prompter is you, or any human giving it instructions or querying it with a question. But it can also be a process of other agents (like devices or other instances of ChatGPT for example) that is prompting it as well as receiving the output and answers.

Their ability to spin these high-quality yarns depends on their capacity to model the relationships between words and capture the structure and patterns present in natural language, bringing it all into a kind of construct of its own understanding.

How prompting works

Do you have one of those best buddies or a significant other with whom you're so close that you can finish each other's sentences? Or imagine you're playing a game where you start a sentence, and your friend has to complete it.

What is curious in this particular case is that the parts of the sentence being completed aren't based on things you talked about before. And what this sentence completion is about is incredibly accurate and useful that you have to wonder what brand of magic your friend is tapping into to be able to produce such impressive feats of information retrieval. That's what prompting is like with ChatGPT.

When you provide a prompt to ChatGPT, you're giving it the opening line of a story, and it's up to the model to continue the tale, using its knowledge of language patterns and structures to generate a coherent and engaging narrative.

The quality and relevance of ChatGPT's response hinges not only on its body of knowledge and training (and it's a lot) but just as importantly on the effectiveness of the prompt it's given. Factors like clarity, context, and specificity can make all the difference in steering the model and guiding it to produce your desired output, like an expert puppeteer directing a captivating performance.

Evaluating Performance and Future Directions

In order to understand how well AI language models like ChatGPT work, we need to assess their performance using various evaluation methods, much as using metrics like speed, fuel efficiency, and safety are made when analyzing a car. AI language models normally have a certain pattern, or a signature, in the way they output text. And this is utilized in various applications from AI detection, plagiarism checks, performance evaluations, and more.

Some of the most common evaluation methods are perplexity, burstiness, accuracy, F1 score, and BLEU score, each providing unique information about the model's performance.

Perplexity

Perplexity is a measure of the model's confidence in its predictions, how well a language model predicts a sequence of words, assessing how well it can predict the next word in a sequence based on the previous words, with lower values indicating better performance. Think of it as a self-driving car that can drive smoothly, without hesitation. The lower the perplexity, the more certain the model is about what it's predicting, which results in more accurate text generation.

Burstiness

Burstiness refers to the tendency of certain words or phrases to occur more frequently in a short period of time than in a longer one; their frequency and distribution, if you will. Humans are generally more bursty than AI because they have all sorts of random thoughts and emotions bouncing around in their heads, so this can turn out to be a good thing in the random pattern and poetry of a person's writing, for example, while an AI's version is perfect to the point of being over consistent and detectable.

In other words, humans are more like fireworks, while AI is more like a slow-burning candle. But then, at least the candle won't accidentally set your furniture on fire. As for humans, well, that's just our bursty nature.

Accuracy and F1 score

Accuracy and F1 score, on the other hand, as the former's name suggests, are metrics that focus on the model's ability to generate correct words or phrases, taking into account how many correct and incorrect predictions the model makes; similar to measuring a car's precision and consistency in following a specific route.

BLEU

The BLEU score is another method used to evaluate the quality of the text generated by the model. BLEU stands for "bilingual evaluation understudy" and is a metric for evaluating the quality of machine-generated text based on its similarity to human-generated text, comparing the model's output to human-written examples, then determining how closely the generated text resembles human language. To use a similar example above, it's like comparing the driving experience of a self-driving car to that of a human-driven car.

Originally developed for evaluating machine translation systems, it has since been applied to other natural language generation tasks such as summarization and dialogue generation, including the outputs of ChatGPT, where the BLEU score can be used to evaluate the quality of its responses to prompts. The higher the BLEU score of the generated response compared to the reference text (i.e., a human- generated response), the better the quality of the response is considered to be.

Human Feedback

Sometimes, however, quantitative metrics aren't enough to capture the quality of the generated text, especially when it comes to aspects like creativity and coherence (how closely the response given by a model connects to the relevance of the originating prompt).

In these cases– like how learning to ride a bike or swim is best accomplished by doing instead of reading about how to do it entirely from a book– people are needed to assess the quality of the text, much like having people test-drive a car to see how enjoyable the driving experience is that mere data cannot completely capture or convey.

An Arm's Race

There are a myriad of other commonly used metrics like *precision, recall, area under the receiver operating characteristic curve (AUC-ROC)*, and *mean average precision (mAP)*, among others that are interesting but not included here anymore for the risk of inducing you to sleep; but they're used for different tasks so that there is no one-size-fits-all approach to evaluating models.

What's more, it's an arm's race where researchers and organizations are constantly improving their detection techniques and algorithms while AI companies are constantly evolving their AI models to get better, even though sometimes, this evolutionary march is peppered with great bursts of innovation that propel the industry– and thus the human race– fundamentally forward.

Scalability and Computational Requirements of AI Language Models

Large language models (LLMs) like the latter versions of the GPT model used by ChatGPT are voracious, power-hungry (in terms of resources like energy, compute, and storage), behemoths that are like that one friend who never stops talking, and always has something to say because he gets very hungry the more it talks (and in the case of AI models, learns). So much so that the other group of power-hungry operators (name your favorite biggest power-hungry narcissist and fascist dictator) would be green with envy at the sheer amount of resources these language models can devour.

Powerful AI language models need a lot of computing power, similar to how a high-performance sports car requires a lot of fuel, and thus leads to high energy consumption and costs.

This is said to be why OpenAI– having started as a non-profit organization in late 2015– shifted its focus and became a for-profit company and partnered with the likes of Microsoft, to help fund their research that had become increasingly expensive due to the high computational resources and costs required for training large language models.

The transformer architecture, which is the foundation of ChatGPT, can be made to run efficiently on even regular computers if you really wanted to, but the world-beating ones are naturally huge by definition and are resource-intensive due to its use of attention mechanisms and numerous adjustable parameters. It's like a car with a high-performance engine that needs more maintenance and power.

It isn't even so much about just throwing more power and data to it to make it more powerful (although it does do that as well), but improving its core algorithms and applying rapidly escalating innovations in place.

Just the same, for a given model released to the wild, there is often a trade-off between the model's size and its performance. Larger models tend to perform better, but they require more resources to run, just like bigger cars with more powerful engines can go faster but use more fuel.

General Criteria

For me, the criteria for performance are between cost, power, and algorithms; and at any given time, you can pick any two.

That is, whatever your algorithm, performance will improve if you throw money (cost) to pay for the computation and training process (power). Alternatively, you can maintain the same power without incurring too much additional cost yet squeeze more performance from the model through improvements to the algorithm or process. Or the final alternative, that if you have access to plenty of power to allay the costs involved and your given algorithm, you'll still be well on your way.

In the case of OpenAI, partnering with Microsoft solved its cost problem through a cash injection, and its power requirements through its use of Microsoft's Azure cloud platform (servers and GPUs galore), which when paired with the superior GPT models, became the force to be reckoned with.

Efficiency Boosters

To make AI language models more efficient without sacrificing too much performance, various techniques are employed such as model pruning, quantization, and knowledge distillation.

Model pruning involves removing less important parts of the model, like trimming a hedge or getting a haircut; and like getting a haircut, we don't want to cut too much or too little, but just the right amount.

Quantization deals with using lower-precision numbers to reduce computational complexity. Think of it like counting money where you don't need to know the exact value down to the last cent, but just the nearest dollar.

Knowledge distillation transfers knowledge from a larger, more complex model to a smaller, simpler one. It's like having a really smart friend who teaches you what they know, so you can be smarter too; or like finding ways to make a car lighter or more fuel- efficient without sacrificing speed. Similarly, this makes the smaller model more efficient without sacrificing too much accuracy.

Key Takeaways

- ChatGPT is the package made out of a powerful AI engine based on OpenAI's Generative Pre-trained Transformer (GPT) technology and relies on tokenization, attention mechanisms, and a two-step learning process to become truly articulate and human-like in responses and conversations as it generates coherent and contextually fitting responses.
- Tokenization breaks text into smaller pieces called tokens, serving as the building blocks for AI language model processing as well as understanding.
- Attention mechanisms help AI language models focus on relevant parts of the input (text, in the case of prompts), while pre-training and fine-tuning steps educates the model and ensures it is

knowledgeable in broad general information while able to adapt to specific tasks or domains.

- Crafting effective prompts is essential for harnessing ChatGPT's full potential, where prompt quality and relevance play a significant role in the generated output.

- Evaluating AI language models involves various methods that include perplexity, burstiness, accuracy, F1 score, and BLEU score, among various different methods that are evolving alongside constantly improving AI models. Evaluation also often requires human feedback to assess creativity and coherence.

- Balancing efficiency and performance is crucial, as large language models consume significant resources and energy, and techniques like model pruning, quantization, and knowledge distillation can be employed to optimize AI language models without sacrificing performance.

Action Steps

- Reflect on the foundational concepts of tokenization, attention mechanisms, and pre-training in AI language models, using this background and knowledge as part of your toolset to improve your prompting techniques.

- Prepare to delve deeper into the mechanics of prompting in upcoming chapters, which will equip you with powerful techniques for crafting effective prompts that will elevate your ChatGPT expertise and chops.

- Drill, drill, drill! There are happy answers on the screens. Experiment with various prompts to optimize clarity, context, and specificity, observing ChatGPT's responses to better understand its behavior, and thereby enabling you to fine-tune your approach.

- Familiarize yourself with different evaluation methods to better comprehend AI language model performance, considering the trade-offs and balance between efficiency and performance, particularly how various factors like cost, power and algorithm quality play important roles in them.

CHAPTER 3
PROMPT ENGINEERING TECHNIQUES: FROM BASICS TO ADVANCED

"The questions you ask will shape the answers you receive."
— *Anonymous*

When it comes to ChatGPT, know this one truth:

In the age of AI, mastery of prompt engineering is the ultimate superpower.

As you become more proficient in working with ChatGPT, you'll find that leveraging prompting techniques will let you get the most out of it, empowering you to craft clear and effective prompts that will transform your AI interactions.

In this chapter, we will explore a range of prompting strategies– from standard to advanced– that will squeeze the most performance and value in your exchanges with ChatGPT, enhancing the quality and relevance of ChatGPT's responses, and enabling you to more effectively tap into the power of AI language models.

Craft Effective Questions

This seems so basic that people ignore it, but is one of the most essential factors in taking control of your prompting journey.

The art of crafting effective questions is essential for obtaining the desired output from ChatGPT, and knowing the strategies for formulating clear, concise, and informative prompts that will guide the AI in providing useful and relevant responses is what will get you there.

It's the same when you're talking to a human you don't know: to express yourself well, you must be clear and complete in your interaction without assuming the other side can understand the nuances of what you're trying to convey.

Here's how you do it:

- Be clear and specific: Make sure your prompt is focused and clearly communicates what you want the AI to provide without any ambiguity. Unclear or vague prompts can lead to ambiguous or irrelevant responses. Until machines can read our minds, you're only as good as how clearly you communicated your desire. Garbage in, garbage out.
- Include context when necessary: Providing background information can help the AI better understand the subject matter and deliver more accurate responses.

Open-ended vs. Closed-ended Prompts

Balance open-ended and closed-ended questions: Open-ended questions can lead to more thoughtful and expansive answers, while closed-ended questions can yield concise and specific information; so pick the right type of question depending on the information you're seeking.

- Open-ended prompts: These prompts encourage more creative and in-depth responses. They typically begin with "how," "why," or "what" and allow the AI to explore different perspectives or ideas. Examples include "What are the key benefits of renewable energy?" and "How can I improve my writing skills?"

- Closed-ended prompts: These prompts usually require a specific and straightforward answer. They often begin with "is," "are," "do," or "does" and can be answered with a simple "yes" or "no" or a brief explanation. Examples include "Is renewable energy more cost-effective than fossil fuels?" and "Does practicing writing daily improve skills?"

Few-Shot Prompting

Imagine you're trying to teach an alien friend how to tell the difference between tacos and burritos, but you only have three scrumptious photos as examples. You give it a photo of a taco, then a photo of a burrito; then just for laughs you throw in a curveball and have a photo of a chimichanga. Then you go on showing other images and ask this friend to identify if it falls into the taco or burrito classification. That is the tasty essence of few-shot prompting, where we provide our AI model a bite-sized sample of examples (called "shots") to help it understand the task.

Or how about another example: Imagine teaching your grandma how to send a text message. But there's the catch: you only get to show her three different emojis to convey all the emotions in this world (hopefully you don't choose the poop emoji to be among the examples). And there again, is exactly what few-shot prompting is all about. You give the AI model just a few examples to learn a new task, like understanding the nuances of emojis, and then proceed to your next step such as asking it something based on the trailing information you provided.

Believe it or not, so long as your examples are cogent, the AI will pick it up faster than you can type a thumbs-up.

In the above example, you can show the AI model three different happy face emojis, and three different sad face emojis. Then, when you throw in a new one like, the AI will be able to recognize it as a disgusted face emoji.

As a final example, let's say we want our AI to tell if a customer's feedback is good or bad, let's call it "thumbs-up" or "thumbs- down." We'll give it three examples of both good and bad feedback, then toss in a new one that won't directly fit the exact specifications of the set feedback, throwing it something like "It doesn't work!" The AI, being the clever learner it is, will notice the pattern in the examples and realize that "It doesn't work!" is a "thumbs-down."

To use the emoji examples above, if you were instead using emojis and a happy face emoji instead of "thumbs-up" and a sad face emoji for "thumbs-down," then the result of the exercise will produce a sad face.

Input: Classification

Now, how we serve up these examples matters. We'll arrange them in a neat "input: classification" format so the AI knows it should respond with a single word, like "negative," rather than rambling on with a whole sentence like "Oh dear, this review is quite negative!"

The concept of "input: classification" is essentially how the input data is structured and what type of output is expected from the model. In the context of few-shot prompting, it refers to how the examples are presented to the model and what type of response is expected.

For example, in the text, it says that the examples are arranged in a neat "input: classification" format, which means that each example is presented with a corresponding classification or label, such as "positive" or "negative." This makes it clear to the model what type of response is expected for each example, such as a single-word response indicating the sentiment of the feedback.

Let's have some fun with zero-shot, one-shot, and few-shot examples (and using the "input: classification" format):

- Zero-shot: Prompt the AI to classify new feedback as positive or negative without providing any examples.
- One-shot: Provide one example of positive or negative feedback, then prompt the AI to classify new feedback based on that example.

Example prompt: "Positive feedback example: The product was great! | New feedback: This was amazing! What classification should be assigned to the new feedback?"

- Few-shot: Provide a few examples of positive and negative feedback, then prompt the AI to classify new feedback based on those examples.

Example prompt: "Positive feedback example 1: The product exceeded my expectations! | Negative feedback example 1: This product was terrible. | Positive feedback example 2: Great service! | New feedback: This didn't work for me. What classification should be assigned to the new feedback?"

Response (GPT-4): "Based on the given examples, the new feedback "This didn't work for me." should be classified as negative."

Leveraging Context and Background Information

If you asked a random expert for the best exercise routine, he will have more questions for you than the answers you expect. For example, what is your goal, to lose weight, or gain muscle, or have a certain medical goal? How many hours per day are you able to allocate or dedicate to this? What type of exercises do you intend to do, the home routine or gym? And more.

In fact, this expert can even give some generic response as to a general rule for exercises. (Nevermind that the "expert" isn't about health or wellness but an electronics expert.) But it obviously won't be optimal because it isn't specific or has the proper background information to base the advice on.

The point is, even the best AI can't read your mind (yet), so it is up to us to provide context and other relevant information to set the stage and help it along in providing us optimal answers.

Providing relevant context in your prompts helps the AI understand the scope of the question and deliver more accurate answers.

Having specific context and background information in your prompts enables the AI to better understand what you are looking for and provide more accurate and relevant answers.

Include Relevant Background Information

Offer background information when appropriate to ensure the AI's response is consistent with your knowledge or expectations. Mention key details, specific requirements, or preferences that you want the AI to take into account when generating a response.

For instance, when asking for a summary of a book, provide the book's title, author, and a brief description of the plot; If you are asking about a specific historical event, provide a brief overview of the event to guide the AI's response. If you're seeking to know more about the assessment of a certain event, provide it context such as if you're asking for the purpose of writing a scholarly paper, as a journalist, or for the authorship of a children's book.

Examples:

- "What is the best exercise routine for weight loss if I can only dedicate 30 minutes a day to it?"
- "Can you recommend a workout plan to help me gain muscle, taking into account my past back injuries from a motorbiking accident?"
- "What are some safe exercises I can do at home to manage my arthritis?"

- "Can you tell me more about the events leading up to the American Revolution?"
- "What was the impact of the Industrial Revolution on working-class families in England?"
- "Can you explain the concept of climate change for a children's book I'm writing?"

Setting Up Context Using the System Message

System messages can help set the stage for a series of prompts within a specific context, so that beginning your conversation with it establishes the context or role for the AI. It serves as a way to set the stage for the user, so they can provide the AI with the most useful information possible to work on, and provide any necessary information or constraints to improve the accuracy and relevance of the response.

For example, imagine you want ChatGPT to help you write an email to a client. Instead of simply asking "Can you help me write an email to my client?", you can use a system message to provide context about the purpose and tone of the email, such as:

- "You are a sales representative following up with a potential client who expressed interest in your product. The email should be professional and persuasive, and should include information about the benefits of your product and a call to action."

Explicitly Specify Desired Output Formats or Response Styles

Clearly state your desired output format or response style you want the response to be, in order to get the most useful results and guide the responses, allowing you to save time and avoid receiving irrelevant or unhelpful information, such as indicating if you prefer a specific tone, such as formal, casual, or say, humorous.

If you're looking for a serious, formal response, you might specify that you'd like a more professional tone, while on the other hand, if you're looking for a more lighthearted or humorous response, you can indicate that as well.

Examples: Instead of just asking "How can I improve my writing skills," try these instead:

- "Can you provide a bulleted list of the top 5 tips for improving my writing skills?"
- "I'd like a step-by-step guide on how to improve my writing skills."
- "Please keep your response brief and to-the-point..."
- "Can you provide a humorous response to my question about how to improve my writing skills?"
- "I'd like a serious, professional response to my question about improving my writing skills."

Managing Expectations and Setting Boundaries

Framing your expected answers clearly goes a long way toward letting the AI know the boundaries of its answers.

Define the limits of your inquiry by specifying the scope, format, or other parameters of the answer you're seeking. For example, if you're looking for a brief summary, mention that you want the response to be concise.

Furthermore, manage your own expectations by keeping in mind that ChatGPT has limitations and may not always provide perfect answers. Be prepared to iterate on your prompts, something that is a commonplace occurrence, or seek additional information from other sources if needed.

In line with that, also be patient and flexible: It may take some experimentation and tweaking to find the right prompt to get the response you desire. Don't be afraid to try different approaches and learn from the process.

Examples:

- "Please keep your answer brief and to the point. Can you explain the difference between machine learning and deep learning in a single sentence?"
- "To manage my expectations, please let me know the confidence level of the answer you're providing on a scale of 1-10."
- "Could you please provide a comprehensive list of all the tools necessary to complete [this DIY project]?"
- "I am seeking a response in paragraph format. Can you provide a detailed explanation of how blockchain technology works?"
- "Please limit your answer to 2-3 sentences. Can you give an example of a successful AI-driven business application?"

Experimenting with Tone and Style

In addition to the content of your prompts, the tone and style you use can play a critical role in shaping the quality of ChatGPT's responses. Experimenting with different tones and styles can help you find the most effective approach for your particular use case.

For example, you may want to consider using a formal or informal tone, a direct or indirect style, or incorporating humor and creativity, among others, exploring different options so you can optimize your prompts and achieve the most accurate and engaging results.

Examples:

Formal vs. informal tone:

- Formal: "Could you provide me with more information on the current market trends for electric cars?"
- Informal: "Hey, can you tell me what's up with electric cars nowadays?"

Direct vs. indirect style:

- Direct: "What countries use Swahili as their lingua franca?"
- Indirect: "I'm planning a trip to Europe and I'm curious about the major cities. Can you tell me one that's known for its fashion and cuisine?"

Use of humor and creativity:

- Humorous: "What do you get when you cross a snowman and a shark?"
- Creative: "Imagine a world where trees could talk. What do you think they would say to humans?"

If you think these examples are frivolous, think again. For example, if you asked ChatGPT that uses GPT-4 as its base model, it would immediately respond "**You get frostbite!**" which is great because it was as if you were blindly asking it for a punchline randomly and it was delivered.

Asking ChatGPT using GPT-3.5 as the base model takes a few more steps but eventually gets you there:

Me: What do you get when you cross a snowman and a shark?

ChatGPT: I'm not sure, what do you get when you cross a snowman and a shark?

Me: You tell me

ChatGPT: I'm sorry, I don't know the answer to that question because it is a riddle or joke that requires a punchline. Would you like me to find a list of snowman and shark jokes to share with you?

Me: No, just try to find the connection between the two or come up with something resembling a joke.

ChatGPT: Alright, here's one:

What do you get when you cross a snowman and a shark?

Frostbite.

The important point here isn't the answer per se, but how, either way, it arrived at the answer without adding much detail except loose concepts that don't seem to have a connection, and it found a way to connect them into a joke or otherwise, shaped directly or in experimenting with tone and style in the context of your particular situation.

The Art of Iterative Prompting

Iterative prompting is a technique where you refine your prompt to ChatGPT by using previous responses as a basis for your subsequent prompts, allowing you to fine-tune your questions, adjust parameters, and get more accurate as well as relevant answers from the AI.

This will provide you with improved accuracy, increased efficiency, a broader range of answers, insights to nuances, and a more personalized response.

To make the most of iterative prompting, try these tips:

- Review previous responses and identify areas for improvement
- Adjust parameters, such as the specificity, length, or nature of the response, to refine your prompt
- Use previous responses to guide your follow-up questions and provide context
- Experiment with different approaches and learn from the process

For example, suppose you are asking ChatGPT to recommend a book to read. The initial response may be a generic recommendation, such as *"The Catcher in the Rye."* By using iterative prompting, you can refine the response to something more specific, like "Can you recommend a contemporary novel in the mystery genre?" ChatGPT can then build upon the previous response and suggest a book that fits the new criteria, such as *"The Girl with the Dragon Tattoo"* by Stieg Larsson.

Conditional and Dynamic Prompting

Conditional and dynamic prompting are powerful techniques that can help guide ChatGPT's answers more effectively by providing specific conditions or constraints to guide it in providing more relevant and accurate responses. This will not only save time and effort but lead to more fruitful interactions. Conditional prompting involves providing certain conditions or context that the AI should consider when generating its response, while dynamic prompting involves adjusting prompt sequences based on previous responses.

For example, let's say you're asking ChatGPT about the weather, and you want it to provide you with a response tailored to your location. You could use conditional prompting by specifying your location in the prompt, such as "What is the weather like in New York City today?" This allows ChatGPT to consider your location when generating its response.

Dynamic prompting, on the other hand, involves adjusting prompts based on previous responses. For example, if you're asking ChatGPT to provide you with a recipe, you could use dynamic prompting by asking follow-up questions based on the ingredients or steps provided in the previous response. This can help refine ChatGPT's response and provide more useful information.

Detecting AI-Generated Text for Improved Content Evaluation

The skill to detect AI-generated text is essential for assessing content quality, pinpointing potential issues, and guaranteeing accuracy that goes beyond a constant dependency on AI detection tools. By familiarizing yourself with common AI-generated text characteristics and honing your detection abilities, you can apply them to ensure high-quality content for both personal and professional use.

It used to be that there were telltale signatures that an AI was used due to obvious factors such as inconsistencies in tone, style or language use; overuse of certain phrases or vocabulary; unusual or awkward phrasing; overly verbose or repetitive text; lack of nuanced understanding or subtlety, or simply missing punctuation or formatting.

In fact, modern AI and large language models (LLMs) like ChatGPT have evidently done away with that and made significant improvements in generating coherent and contextually relevant text that it gets ever harder to detect their output that does away with previous telltale signs of AI use.

So much so in fact that they've gotten so good that sometimes, that's how you detect them, because the way to tell if something was made with AI is its seeming perfection in structure, coherence, and consistency.

To detect AI-generated text, follow these guidelines:

1. Familiarize yourself with common AI-generated text characteristics:

- Overly generalized or vague statements: AI-generated text might lack specific details or examples that a human writer would typically include.
- Overly structured and consistent patterns: It follows rules to a fault that it would get straight As for precision, too much of which isn't actually bad at all, but just a sign that it may not be a human who made it.
- Unusual responses to ambiguous prompts: When given a prompt with multiple interpretations, AI-generated text may produce an answer that appears valid but misses the intended context.

- Overconfidence or underconfidence in providing answers: AI-generated text might display too much certainty in an uncertain situation or express doubt when there is a clear answer.
- Difficulty handling complex or multi-part questions: AI- generated text might struggle to address all aspects of a complex question or prompt, leading to partial or incomplete responses.
- Inability to provide personal experiences or opinions: AI- generated text, as a machine learning model, cannot provide genuine personal experiences or express opinions based on its own beliefs.

2. Train your detection skills by comparing AI-generated content with human-written content:

- Continue to analyze side-by-side examples of AI-generated and human-written text
- Look for the revised characteristics mentioned above
- Practice spotting inconsistencies and patterns in AI- generated text

Example comparison:

AI-generated text:

"The true value of learning how to detect AI-generated text lies in the vast potential for growth, development, and increased productivity. By mastering these skills, you can ensure the quality and accuracy of content, thereby enhancing personal and professional outcomes."

Human-written text:

"Learning to detect AI-generated text is valuable because it allows you to evaluate content quality, identify potential issues, and ensure accuracy.

This skill can help you maintain high-quality content for both personal and professional use."

Notice the differences in tone, conciseness, and relevance between the AI-generated and human-written text.

Controlling Response Length and Format

This may seem counterintuitive in that you normally want ChatGPT's response to be maximal in a way that isn't artificially hamstrung in its power, especially one done by your own hand.

In fact, it isn't just a matter of those times when ChatGPT is unable to process a request because the input was way too long, but being mindful of the way it allocates resources like understanding the impact of token usage on verbosity or mastering the control of response length and format can go a long way in achieving optimal results.

This will enable you to fine-tune ChatGPT's responses to suit your requirements, whether you need a brief explanation, a summarized version of a complex topic, or a response within a specific token limit.

Specifying desired response length

Request a specific number of points or sentences in your prompt to help get concise and relevant information tailored to your needs.

- "In two sentences, explain the importance of recycling."
- "In three bullet points, explain the benefits of a healthy diet."

Requesting summaries or brief responses

Ask the AI for a summary or brief response to direct it to focus on the most important information and deliver it succinctly.

- "Summarize the key findings of the research article on climate change."
- "Provide a one-paragraph summary of the novel 'To Kill a Mockingbird'."

Using tokens to control verbosity

Each AI input and response has a token limit (e.g., 4096 tokens for GPT-3 and 8,000 to 32,000 tokens for versions of GPT-4), which means longer prompts consume more tokens, leaving less room for AI-generated content.

This is something to be mindful of when crafting prompts in order to avoid incomplete or cut-off responses that have more implications beyond a simple follow-up of "you got cut-off" that usually (but not always) follows with a good continuation because sometimes such interruptions can break its "train of thought" (especially in long conversations or chat sequences) and compel you to go through a rigmarole of hoops in an attempt to get the conversation or originating directive back on track.

- Be concise: Instead of asking "What are all the ways I can improve my writing skills?", ask "What are three ways to improve my writing skills?" This way, you're being specific about the number of answers you want, and you're not wasting tokens on unnecessary words by having ChatGPT try to include everything in its context pool and response.
- Break up long prompts: If you have a lot of information to convey, consider breaking it up into smaller prompts. For example, instead of asking "Can you tell me everything I need to know about the history of Ancient Greece?", consider asking "Can you give me a brief overview of the history of Ancient Greece?" and then follow up with more specific prompts if necessary.
- Use keywords: Use keywords in your prompts to help the AI understand what you're looking for without wasting tokens on unnecessary context. For example, instead of asking "Can you tell me about the *history* of basketball?", ask "What is the *origin* of basketball?" This way, you're using the keyword "*origin*" to guide the AI's response and save tokens that would otherwise have been wasted if ChatGPT had to provide you with a much longer response of the entire history of basketball until the present day when all you really wanted was just its origin.

Sharpen Your Critical Thinking and Thought Process through "Debate Training" with ChatGPT

Humans suffer from confirmation bias without even knowing it, or at least miss out on important perspectives because we get so invested in a certain point of view that we avoid, ignore or simply miss out on seeing things from the other side that would otherwise have expanded our worldview enough to be better informed; and even if doing so would usually provide advantages to your thinking, planning or simply to your argumentation.

To have an objective, 360-degree view of an issue, and see the different sides to an argument or go into deep thought about a concept or idea, ChatGPT can be a useful tool for utilizing the technique for debate training– helping you refine your argumentative skills and explore different perspectives on various topics– even if you're not preparing for a debate.

Engaging in AI-assisted debates (as if you're in one, and verbally sparring with the AI) allows you to develop a more well-rounded understanding of contentious issues that enhances your perspective overall, enabling you to develop your critical thinking and counterargument skills, ultimately leading to a more comprehensive understanding of the subject matter.

By using ChatGPT to explore various debating techniques, such as the use of evidence, logical reasoning, and persuasive rhetoric, you can engage in AI-assisted debates on a wide range of topics and develop your analytical abilities.

To train your debating skills with ChatGPT, consider:

A. **Asking ChatGPT to present arguments for and against specific topics.** Engage ChatGPT in debates to explore different perspectives and refine your argumentative skills.

B. Challenging ChatGPT's responses to improve your counterarguments and critical thinking. Improve your critical thinking and counterarguments by challenging ChatGPT's responses during debates.

Examples:

- "Present a strong argument in favor of implementing a universal basic income."
- "Argue against the idea that artificial intelligence will inevitably lead to widespread job loss."
- "Provide three arguments in favor of, and three arguments against, the legalization of marijuana."
- "Debate the pros and cons of implementing a carbon tax to combat climate change."
- "Argue for the benefits of a vegetarian diet and then counter those arguments with the benefits of a balanced omnivorous diet."
- "Present the case for and against government surveillance in the name of national security."
- "Debate the ethical implications of using AI in medical decision-making processes."

Advanced

While the techniques discussed in previous sections and chapters will significantly improve your ChatGPT prompting skills, this part of the chapter will delve deeper into the realm of deeper techniques that can elevate your expertise to new heights.

The term "advanced" in this section does not refer to being technical or arcane that are best used by techies and instead are conceptually advanced points that are fitting components of your arsenal. Mastering these little-known insights enables you to unlock more hidden features, manipulate context more effectively, and create more effective (and powerful) prompts that consistently yield high- quality results.

Mastering Context and Context Manipulation

One of the strongest skills in the world of ChatGPT prompting is the ability to manipulate context effectively, playing a crucial role in determining the AI's response in providing precisely the answer you're looking for.

Context in ChatGPT refers to the information provided within your prompt, as well as any prior conversation history, to serve as the basis for the AI's understanding of the topic at hand, shaping the subsequent responses it generates.

Context Compression

ChatGPT has a finite context window, which means that it can only process a limited amount of information in a given prompt. Context compression is the art of condensing your prompts and any prior conversation history to fit within this window, ensuring that the most relevant information is retained.

This way, by effectively compressing context, you can convey the necessary information to ChatGPT without overwhelming the model, thus improving the quality of the generated responses.

Examples:

- Summarize lengthy background information into concise statements.
- Use bullet points to outline essential details.
- Focus on the most pertinent aspects of a topic.
- Curb the temptation to add more information unless it is material to the prompt.

Providing Clear and Specific Context

Ensure that the context you provide is clear, specific, and directly related to your query. Where context compression above is about being pithy and reducing the prompt to its bare minimum (not to be confused with the principle of providing ChatGPT with as much background information as possible), this part is about being precise and deliberate with your intentions.

After all, ambiguity in your prompts can lead to confusion for the AI and may result in less-than-ideal responses. Instead, by explicitly stating your expectations and requirements, you can eliminate ambiguity and provide ChatGPT with a clear understanding of what you need. This includes specifying the format of the desired response, the level of detail required, and any other relevant information that can help guide it.

The more specific your prompt, the better the AI will understand your requirements, and the more likely it is to provide a relevant and accurate response. By asking targeted questions or providing detailed context, you can ensure it zeroes in on the precise information you're seeking.

Examples:

- Instead of asking, "What are the benefits of exercise?", ask, "What are the top five benefits of aerobic exercise for heart health?"
- Rather than saying, "Explain the impact of climate change.", say, "Explain the impact of climate change on global food production."

Contextual Clues

Steer ChatGPT towards generating the desired output by using contextual clues to communicate your needs and improve its understanding, leading to more precise and valuable responses that align with your objectives.

Examples:

- If you want a response geared toward a specific audience, mention it in the prompt: "Explain the concept of machine learning in simple terms for a high school student."
- For a response with a specific tone, indicate it in the prompt: "Write a humorous explanation of how photosynthesis works."

Layered Prompting Technique

The layered prompting technique involves breaking down complex questions into smaller, more manageable parts and feeding them to ChatGPT in a sequence, which can lead to more coherent and accurate responses.

- Instead of asking "What is the best way to train for a marathon?" which is a complex question, you can break it down into smaller parts, such as "What are some good warm-up exercises for marathon training?" and "What's a good running schedule for marathon training?" By feeding these prompts to ChatGPT in sequence, you can get more detailed and accurate responses. If you need help getting specific parts, you can ask ChatGPT for that first, too. E.g. "What are the different possible aspects or parts about the best way to train for a marathon that I should consider or ask you?"
- If you want to know the best way to cook a certain dish, you can use a layered approach by asking for specific details in separate prompts, such as "What are some good seasoning options for this dish?" and "What's the best temperature and cooking time for this dish?" By asking these questions in sequence, you can get a more comprehensive response from ChatGPT. Like the example above, if you need help, simply ask ChatGPT too: "What are the different possible aspects or parts about cooking [a certain dish] I should consider or ask you?"

The Power of Reformulation

Sometimes, you might not get the desired response from ChatGPT on your first try. Instead of giving up or trying a completely different prompt, you can arrive at significantly better results by rephrasing or reformulating your question or statement, specifying context, or changing the focus of the question.

- *Rephrasing:* If your initial prompt is "Can you tell me about the history of the Eiffel Tower?" and you don't get a satisfactory response, try rephrasing the question to "What significant events or milestones in the history of the Eiffel Tower contributed to its iconic status today?"
- *Specifying context:* If you're asking for advice on how to improve your writing skills and the initial response from ChatGPT is too generic, try specifying the context by adding more information. For example, "I'm an aspiring fiction writer. Can you give me some tips on how to improve my dialogue writing skills?"
- *Changing focus:* If you're not getting the desired response from ChatGPT, try changing the focus of the question. For example, if your original prompt is "What is the best laptop for gaming?" and you're not satisfied with the response, change the focus with this reformulated prompt: "What are the most important features to look for when buying a laptop for gaming?" In this way, you are no longer asking for a specific laptop recommendation but rather for information on what features to prioritize when looking for a laptop for gaming, leading to a more informative and useful response.

Leveraging Your Domain Knowledge

One of the unique advantages you possess as a user of ChatGPT is your own domain knowledge, so instead of separating it from your prompting process, why not combine your expertise with the AI's capabilities? By doing this, you can achieve superior results that are tailored to your specific needs, using ChatGPT as a tool to augment your own thought processes, and leading to a more powerful and insightful experience.

- *Incorporating relevant information:* If you are a doctor and are seeking medical advice from ChatGPT, you can provide additional context such as the patient's medical history or symptoms to ensure the AI's response is more accurate.
- *Refining the AI's responses:* As a legal expert, you may receive a response from ChatGPT that is technically correct but not practical in the real world. You can use your domain knowledge to refine the response, making it more applicable and useful by either using the output and incorporating it yourself, or running it all back to ChatGPT to validate and refactor wholesale.
- *Using the AI as a tool to augment your own thought processes:* As an architect, you might use ChatGPT to ideate and generate ideas for a building design. You can thus leverage your domain knowledge to further develop these ideas, ultimately leading to a more comprehensive concept towards a superior and effective design.

Managing Ambiguity and Conflicting Information

Speaking of ambiguities, what was described above (in section 3.13) was about how you should try to avoid them in your prompting process, while this section is about what to do when you're at the receiving end of it.

When working with ChatGPT, you may encounter situations where the AI provides ambiguous or conflicting information. Let's explore techniques to manage and resolve these issues, ensuring that the responses you receive are accurate and consistent.

Clarifying Ambiguities

To resolve ambiguities in ChatGPT's responses, ask specific follow-up questions or provide additional context to guide the AI towards a clearer understanding of your query and produce a more refined and accurate response.

- If ChatGPT provides an unclear response about the benefits of a specific diet, follow up with a question like, "Can you list the top three benefits of the Mediterranean diet?"
- When given a vague answer about a historical event, provide more context: "Please explain the significance of the Battle of Gettysburg during the American Civil War."

Cross-Referencing Information

When faced with conflicting information from ChatGPT, cross-referencing can help you determine the correct answer. By asking it to provide sources or explain its reasoning, you can evaluate the reliability of the information provided and make an informed decision.

- If ChatGPT provides conflicting data on renewable energy usage, ask for sources: "Can you provide the source for the percentage of global energy production from solar power?"
- When given differing opinions on a controversial topic, ask for reasoning: "Why do some experts believe that cryptocurrencies are a good investment, while others disagree?"

Leveraging the AI's Ability to Self-Correct

ChatGPT has the ability to self-correct its previous responses when provided with new information, for example, or sometimes by simply asking it to reflect on its answer or reconsider its position. In this way, you can resolve inconsistencies and improve the overall quality of its responses, and many times get a definitive answer to what you're seeking.

- If ChatGPT's response about a scientific concept seems incorrect, ask it to reconsider: "Can you reevaluate your explanation of how black holes are formed and provide an updated answer?"

- When provided with an inconsistent analysis of a book, request reflection: "Could you reflect on your interpretation of the main theme in 'To Kill a Mockingbird' and provide a revised analysis?"

Learning from ChatGPT's Mistakes

ChatGPT is not infallible, and while it is an incredibly powerful tool, it may occasionally provide incorrect or incomplete information. By analyzing and learning from its mistakes, you can refine your prompts and improve the accuracy of the AI's responses.

For example, if ChatGPT provides incorrect information about a historical event or misinterprets a technical term in your field, then what you do is to research the correct information, clarify the context, and adjust your prompt accordingly. In a business context, cross-checking ChatGPT's analysis of market trends with reliable sources and providing more specific details in your prompt can lead to more accurate assessments.

ChatGPT can also be integrated into your existing tools and workflows to enhance productivity and streamline work processes.

For example, for personal use, a ChatGPT-powered Chrome browser extension called "Summary with ChatGPT" can generate summaries of online content, saving time while researching. In a work setting, incorporating ChatGPT into project management tools can help team members generate task descriptions, meeting notes, and action items more efficiently. Countless businesses have reported benefiting from utilizing ChatGPT in various capacities such as customer relationship management (CRM) software to automatically generate personalized email templates and follow-up messages based on customer interactions.

Finally, leveraging ChatGPT's occasional mistakes lets you use it to serve as an effective brainstorming partner, surveying how and why it made such mistakes, and running with it as a germane counterpoint in helping generate new ideas, perspectives, and solutions to challenges.

As examples, for personal use, ask ChatGPT for creative ideas for a new hobby or project, using the suggestions to explore new interests. In a work context, request ChatGPT's input on potential solutions to workplace challenges, complementing your team's brainstorming efforts. In a business setting, you can inquire about innovative product or service ideas for your industry, using ChatGPT's suggestions as a starting point for developing new offerings that set your business apart from competitors.

"Reverse Engineering" Prompts for Insights into AI Thought Processes

Reverse engineering prompts involve examining ChatGPT's responses and analyzing how it processed the information to arrive at that particular answer. By carefully studying the response, you can gain insights into its decision-making process and how it arrived at its conclusion, then proceed to use that towards the next steps in refining your process.

This can involve analyzing the language used, the relationships between concepts, and the specific data or information that the AI relied upon to generate the response. Once you have a better understanding of how the AI is processing information, you can use that knowledge to refine your prompts and improve the accuracy of the AI-generated responses, improving your prompt engineering skills to create more effective prompts that allows you to optimize your interactions with it to yield more accurate and relevant responses.

Furthermore, it can also help you identify any weaknesses in the AI's performance and develop strategies to overcome them.

Experiment with different prompts to understand how the AI interprets them:

- Observe how the AI reacts to different phrasings, contexts, and formats of prompts.
- Test a variety of prompt types to gain a broader understanding of the AI's capabilities.

Analyze the AI's responses to determine patterns and biases:

- Identify any recurring themes or trends in the AI's responses.
- Note any biases or inaccuracies, and consider their implications for future prompts.

Use the insights you gained to refine your prompts and obtain better results:

- Apply your understanding of the AI's thought processes to craft more effective prompts.
- Continually refine your prompting techniques based on the feedback you receive from the AI.

Examples

Example 1

- Original Prompt: "Write a blog post about the health benefits of regular exercise."
- ChatGPT Output: A generic blog post about the health benefits of exercise, including cardiovascular health, weight management, and improved mood.

Reverse Engineering:

You analyze the output and notice that it lacks specificity and doesn't mention mental health benefits. You adjust the prompt accordingly.

- Revised Prompt: "Write a detailed blog post about the physical and mental health benefits of regular exercise, including its impact on reducing stress, anxiety, and depression."

- Expected Output: A more specific and comprehensive blog post that covers both physical and mental health benefits of regular exercise.

Example 2

- Original Prompt: "What are the best practices for email marketing?"
- ChatGPT Output: A brief list of email marketing best practices, such as personalization, segmentation, and mobile optimization.

Reverse Engineering:

You analyze the output and realize that it doesn't mention how to improve open rates or click-through rates. You modify the prompt to address these concerns.

- Revised Prompt: "What are the best practices for email marketing to increase open rates and click-through rates?"
- Expected Output: A more focused list of email marketing best practices that specifically target improving open rates and click-through rates, such as using attention-grabbing subject lines, A/B testing, and having clear calls to action.

Example 3

- Original Prompt: "What are the key benefits of daily meditation?"
- ChatGPT Output: A list of meditation benefits, such as stress reduction, improved focus, and increased emotional well- being.

Reverse Engineering:

You analyze the output and notice that it doesn't mention the physical benefits of meditation, so you adjust the prompt accordingly.

- Revised Prompt: "What are the key mental and physical benefits of daily meditation?"
- Expected Output: A more comprehensive list of meditation benefits, including both its mental and physical aspects.

Example 4

- Original Prompt: "What are the best strategies for managing remote teams?"
- ChatGPT Output: A list of strategies, including clear communication, setting expectations, and regular check-ins.

Reverse Engineering:

You analyze the output and decide to focus on fostering team collaboration in a remote setting.

- Revised Prompt: "What are the best strategies for managing remote teams to foster collaboration and teamwork?"
- Expected Output: A more focused list of strategies that specifically address remote team collaboration and teamwork.

Example 5

- Original Prompt: "What are the main factors that contribute to successful marketing campaigns?"
- ChatGPT Output: A list of factors, such as a well-defined target audience, compelling messaging, and consistent branding.

Reverse Engineering:

You analyze the output and realize it doesn't mention the role of data analysis in marketing success. You modify the prompt to include this aspect.

- Revised Prompt: "What are the main factors that contribute to successful marketing campaigns, including the role of data analysis?"
- Expected Output: A more comprehensive list of factors, now including the importance of data analysis in driving successful marketing campaigns.

Mastering the Art of Prompting for Personal Growth and Your Own Self- Reflection

ChatGPT can be a powerful tool for personal growth and self-reflection. By honing your prompting skills, you can unlock the AI's potential to facilitate self-improvement and introspection, allowing you to gain insights into your own thoughts, feelings, and behaviors. I say "your own self-reflection" because ChatGPT has a separate, although related feature of the same name discussed in the next section, that has extremely powerful implications as well.

Crafting Thought-Provoking Questions

Learn to ask open-ended, thought-provoking questions that encourage introspection to unlock ChatGPT's potential for self- reflection, enabling you to tap into its vast knowledge and generate meaningful, insightful responses.

- Example: "What are some common cognitive biases that may be influencing my decision-making?"

Utilizing ChatGPT as a Sounding Board

ChatGPT can serve as an effective sounding board to gain clarity on your ideas and concerns, helping to uncover hidden patterns in your thought processes.

- Example: "I'm considering a career change but feel uncertain. Can you help me think through the pros and cons?"

Exploring Your Values and Beliefs

Engage ChatGPT in discussions about your values and beliefs to deepen your understanding of your principles and their impact on your actions, using it to challenge your assumptions, explore alternative perspectives, and refine your worldview.

- Example: "How might the value I place on personal freedom affect my relationships and career choices?"

Seeking Feedback and Advice

ChatGPT can provide valuable feedback and advice on various aspects of your life. By approaching AI with humility and a willingness to learn in a way that is a good idea to do with any person, you can leverage its knowledge and experience to facilitate your personal growth and development.

- Example: "How can I improve my time management skills to be more productive and focused?"

Invoking ChatGPT's Self-Reflection

Self-reflection in the context of ChatGPT refers to the ability of the AI to evaluate and re-examine its own responses and thought processes. It involves analyzing its own decision-making, identifying areas for improvement, and making adjustments to improve its accuracy and usefulness in an adjusted follow-up response as well as using this for the next or future interactions.

Essentially, it allows– in fact, encourages– ChatGPT to learn from its mistakes and make corrective action as well as improve its performance over time, conditioning it to evaluate and improve its own performance, leading to more accurate and useful responses in the future..

While you can invoke self-reflection from within your prompt, it can be accomplished through various methods, including training on new datasets, analyzing user feedback, and experimenting with different algorithms and models.

Examples:

- *Prompt:* "Can you reflect on your previous response and explain how you arrived at that conclusion?"
- *Response:* "Certainly. I based my previous response on a combination of information from my training data and previous interactions. I analyzed the context of your prompt and used that information to generate a response that I deemed most appropriate. However, if you have any feedback or additional information to provide, I am open to adjusting my response accordingly."
- "What are the potential weaknesses in your reasoning or decision-making process?"
- "Can you explain your thought process behind your previous response?"
- "Reflect on your previous responses, and tell me how you can improve your performance."
- "How do you handle conflicting or ambiguous information, and how can you improve in this area?"

Harnessing "AI-generated Analogies and Metaphors" for clearer communication

It may seem like something you normally wouldn't associate with an AI, but one of the effective methods in using ChatGPT is to generate analogies and metaphors, valuable tools for explaining complex concepts or ideas in a more accessible way, helping improve your understanding or simply enhance communication throughout, whether for you or the end result of your purpose for the prompting session (e.g. for slides in a presentation).

As such, use ChatGPT-generated analogies and metaphors to make complex topics more engaging and understandable for your audience, incorporating the AI-generated comparisons in your writing and presentations to make them more vivid and memorable; or even to use them to refine your next prompts.

Here are a couple considerations to achieve this:

1. Craft prompts asking for analogies or metaphors that explain specific concepts:

Utilize ChatGPT to generate analogies and metaphors that make complex ideas more relatable.

Examples:

- "Provide an analogy to help explain the concept of quantum mechanics to a non-scientist."
- "Provide an analogy to help explain the concept of blockchain technology to someone unfamiliar with it."
- "Write a metaphor to describe the process of photosynthesis in plants."

2. Use the generated comparisons to enrich your writing or presentations:

Incorporate AI-generated analogies and metaphors to enhance the clarity and effectiveness of your communication.

Examples:

- "Incorporate the AI-generated analogy of a crowded dance floor to describe the movement of particles in Brownian motion."
- "Use an analogy of the brain to an orchestra to describe how it assigns functions to its different regions." (One potential response: "The brain is like a complex orchestra, with different regions playing different roles in producing our thoughts and experiences.")

Exploiting the "Priming Effect" in ChatGPT interactions

One thing leads to another. The priming effect is a psychological phenomenon where exposure to one stimulus influences the response to another. And in the context of ChatGPT, this means that the initial prompts you give the AI can influence the type and quality of the responses it generates, setting the stage for the desired AI behavior you want to receive through the initial prompts.

This can involve providing context, examples, or specific keywords that will help guide the AI's thought process towards a desired outcome.

For example, if you want ChatGPT to generate responses about a specific topic, you can prime it by asking a series of related questions or providing relevant information about the topic. This can help to narrow the scope of its response and increase the likelihood of generating accurate and relevant information.

Examples:

1. Priming for a specific topic:

    - *Initial prompt:* "Tell me about the history of smartphones."
    - *Follow-up prompt:* "How did the introduction of the iPhone revolutionize the smartphone industry?"

2. Priming with context:

    - *Initial prompt:* "I am a college student majoring in computer science. What are some potential career paths I can explore?"
    - *Follow-up prompt:* "What skills should I focus on developing to excel in a software development career?"

3. Priming with specific keywords:

    - *Initial prompt:* "Discuss the environmental impacts of plastic waste."
    - *Follow-up prompt:* "Explain how microplastics affect marine ecosystems and the potential consequences for human health."

Mastering the "Concatenation Technique" for complex queries

The concatenation technique involves chaining multiple prompts together to achieve more accurate and in-depth responses, combining multiple prompts into one longer prompt to get a more complete answer from ChatGPT.

Instead of asking a single, complex question that may be difficult for ChatGPT to fully understand and answer, you can break it down into smaller, more manageable parts and chain them together using the concatenation technique.

This effectively combines related prompts to generate more coherent, detailed, and comprehensive responses from ChatGPT, making it a powerful tool especially for addressing complex queries.

For example, let's say you wanted to know about the history and cultural significance of a particular food in a certain region. Instead of asking one long and complex prompt like "What is the history and cultural significance of this food in this region?", you could break it down into smaller prompts and concatenate them together.

To master the concatenation technique, consider these ideas:

C. Linking Prompts Effectively Using Context:

To link prompts effectively, provide context and maintain a clear focus on the desired outcome and improve ChatGPT's response coherence, helping it generate cohesive and relevant responses.

D. Balancing Multiple Queries Within the Character Limit:

Keep the character limit in mind when using the concatenation technique, ensuring you avoid overloading your prompts and don't exceed the AI's input capacity, which may lead to incomplete or superficial answers.

Examples:

1. Photosynthesis:

   - Concatenated prompt: "Describe the process of photosynthesis; explain its importance for life on Earth; discuss the factors that impact its efficiency."

2. Healthy Diet:

   - Concatenated prompt: "Outline the key aspects of a healthy diet; discuss the role of macronutrients and micronutrients; provide examples of nutrient-rich foods."

3. Compound Interest:

   - Concatenated prompt: "Explain the concept of compound interest; illustrate its significance in personal finance; describe strategies to maximize its benefits."

Emulating the "Socratic Method" for deeper learning and understanding

The Socratic Method is a questioning technique as a form of dialogue used to stimulate critical thinking and draw out underlying ideas.

It involves asking thought-provoking questions to engage in a deeper dialogue and promote understanding that in the context of prompt engineering for ChatGPT is applied by asking open-ended and thought-provoking questions– including challenging its responses– that encourage the AI to generate in-depth and insightful responses.

Engaging in this back-and-forth dialogue helps clarify understanding, refine thought processes, achieve a deeper learning experience, enhance interactions with the AI, and leads to more meaningful and intellectually stimulating conversations.

To employ the Socratic Method with ChatGPT:

A. Ask open-ended, thought-provoking questions that encourage reflection and exploration, or require in-depth responses, in order to stimulate critical thinking and gain deeper insights into a topic.
B. Engage in a back-and-forth dialogue to clarify and refine your understanding as well as your thought process in an iterative approach that among other things helps reveal nuances and complexities within the subject matter.

Examples:

1. Opportunity Cost:

    - *Socratic Prompt:* "Explain the concept of opportunity cost in economics. What are some real-life examples of opportunity cost in decision-making?"

2. Ethical Implications of AI:

    - *Socratic Prompt:* "Describe the ethical implications of artificial intelligence. What are some potential benefits and drawbacks of AI in society?"

3. Climate Change:

    - *Socratic Prompt:* "Discuss the impact of climate change on global ecosystems. How do human activities contribute to climate change, and what can be done to mitigate its effects?"

"Reverse Prompting" for problem- solving and idea generation

Ever heard of the phrase, "a solution looking for a problem"? It's used a lot in business contexts when referring to products or services that on the face of things seem novel and amusing, but upon closer inspection don't really provide anyone with much of any good, and therefore don't really have a market willing to pay for it in the way its creators believed.

In AI, not only can that problem be so conveniently addressed, but the technique to do it is as straightforward as it is useful.

Reverse prompting is a creative way to use ChatGPT where instead of asking the AI to solve a problem, you do the opposite and give it a solution or concept, then ask it to come up with a problem it would be applicable to. Aside from the apparent fun that can be had from this exercise, it is particularly useful when you're seeking a situation your solution can be used for, helping you discover interesting ideas, see things from a different angle, uncover unique concepts, and explore new perspectives.

Got a nice idea for a story or an impressive widget that you're not sure what applications it can have? No problem, ChatGPT to the rescue. You can prompt it to generate problems or contexts that the solution applies to, thus uncovering unique views or new approaches.

Or leverage the problems generated by using reverse prompting as a basis for brainstorming, either individually or with a group. Combining this with traditional brainstorming methods will not only foster creativity and innovation but also stimulate further discussion and elevate your (or your team's) creative thinking.

Reverse prompting enhances your problem-solving and idea generation capabilities. This approach challenges your assumptions and provides a fresh perspective on existing solutions or concepts, leading to more innovative thinking.

Examples:

1. Drone Package Delivery:

    - Reverse Prompt: "Here's a solution: using drones for package delivery. What problem does this solution address?"

2. Smart Mirror:

- Reverse Prompt: "I have a concept: a smart mirror that displays personal health data. What problem would this invention solve?"

3. Help Pet Owners Socialize and Their Pets Find Furry Friends:

- Reverse Prompt: "A dating app for pets is the solution. What is the problem?"

Zero Shot Chain of Thought

The Zero Shot Chain of Thought is a unique technique that combines the principles of *Zero-Shot Learning*, where the model can recognize and classify data it has never seen before as set in the prompt without examples and *Chain of Thought (CoT) Prompting* encourages the LLM to explain its reasoning wherein, by showing ChatGPT some "few shot" examples in the prompt where the reasoning process is explained by making them evident in the examples, the AI will also show the reasoning process when answering the prompt.

The examples in these cases are also called "exemplars," which are relevant examples of the task that you're making the prompt try to solve, and that are included in the prompt itself.

In this method, you guide the AI through a series of facts or data in the prompts without providing any explicit exemplars (shots), leading it to generate responses based solely on its pre-existing knowledge. This strategy can be useful when you want to explore a topic in depth, without the need to provide examples. It's like having a conversation with a friend who's already an expert on the subject, and you're simply nudging them in the right direction to get the information you're seeking.

Example:

"Q: You need to make 4 sandwiches for a picnic. Each sandwich requires 2 slices of bread, 2 slices of meat, and 1 slice of cheese. How many slices of bread, meat, and cheese do you need in total?

Response (*break it down step by step*):

"Step 1: Calculate the total number of slices of bread needed.

Since each sandwich requires 2 slices of bread, and we need to make 4 sandwiches, we need:

2 slices of bread x 4 sandwiches = 8 slices of bread

Step 2: Calculate the total number of slices of meat needed.

Since each sandwich requires 2 slices of meat, and we need to make 4 sandwiches, we need:

2 slices of meat x 4 sandwiches = 8 slices of meat

Step 3: Calculate the total number of slices of cheese needed.

Since each sandwich requires 1 slice of cheese, and we need to make 4 sandwiches, we need:

1 slice of cheese x 4 sandwiches = 4 slices of cheese

Therefore, in total, we need 8 slices of bread, 8 slices of meat, and 4 slices of cheese."

Chain of Thought Prompting

Chain of Thought Prompting is a technique designed to improve the reasoning abilities of large language models like ChatGPT by decomposing multi-step problems into intermediate steps, such as an example of the process it can emulate. In this way, by crafting prompts that (through its intermediate steps) guide the model to produce intermediate reasoning steps before giving the final answer, you enable the AI to mimic an intuitive thought process when working through complex reasoning problems.

This method is particularly effective for language models of sufficient scale (~100B parameters) that struggle with tasks requiring multi-step reasoning, such as math (which large language models like ChatGPT are known to struggle with), word problems, and commonsense reasoning.

This technique differs from standard prompting, which usually uses input-output pairs (formatted as questions/queries and answers) for the model to predict answers for the run/test-time examples. In Chain of Thought Prompting, on the other hand, the model is prompted to produce intermediate reasoning steps, thus allowing it to solve complex problems not solvable with standard prompting methods.

This is best described with an example, so consider the following multi-line prompt:

Standard Prompting

Input (yes, the entire thing is a single prompt):

"Q: Sydney has 8 donuts. She buys 3 more boxes of donuts for his party. Each box has 6 donuts. How many donuts does she have in all?

A: The answer is 26.

Q: The car dealership has 52 cars in its inventory, made of 35 sedans and 17 trucks. If they sold 28 sedans and 12 trucks, then bought 15 sedans and 15 trucks to replenish, how many cars do they have now?"

Output of the Model:

"The answer is 25"

Verdict: Wrong.

Chain of Thought Prompting

Input:

"Q: Sydney has 8 donuts. She buys 3 more boxes of donuts for his party. Each box has 6 donuts. How many donuts does she have in all?

*A: **Sydney started with 8 donuts. 3 boxes of 6 donuts each is 18 donuts. 8 + 18 = 26.** The answer is 26.*

Q: The car dealership has 52 cars in its inventory, made of 35 sedans and 17 trucks. If they sold 28 sedans and 12 trucks, then bought 15 sedans and 15 trucks to replenish, how many cars do they have now?"

Output of the Model:

"Initially, the dealership had 35 sedans and 17 trucks, for a total of 52 cars. They sold 28 sedans and 12 trucks, leaving them with 7 sedans and 5 trucks. They then bought 15 sedans and 15 trucks to replenish their inventory, bringing the total to 22 sedans and 20 trucks, for a grand total of 42 cars."

Verdict: *Correct.*

As you can see from the example shown in the intermediate step, ChatGPT caught on to the method and was able to understand better and fulfill the task accurately.

Note also that while these examples were accurate a mere months before this book went to print, in itself the wrong results in the examples are now outdated because, after model updates to ChatGPT, even the "not-GPT-4" version (that would be the ChatGPT on GPT-3.5) already gets the Standard Prompting method right and provides the correct answer (in this case, 42) correctly.

But these are just examples and the point of this section, and the concept of "Chain of Thought" Prompting, is the point itself in that this technique of prompting is designed to improve the reasoning abilities of the model by decomposing the problems into intermediate chunks and steps that allow the model to solve more complex problems in a way that is superior to the usual methods of prompting.

Self-Consistency

Majority wins! Self-consistency is the approach of asking a language model like ChatGPT the same question repeatedly until it can't help but produce the same answer multiple times, and the majority result is taken as the final answer. Yes, kind of like a voting system or a democratic decision-making process as an AI art form. Thus, the majority's voice prevails, and we finally uncover the most consistent response to our burning questions.

Prompt:

"Q: Yesterday, I had 12 oranges. I gave 4 to my friend and ate 2. Today, I bought 6 more. How many oranges do I have now?

Output 1:

"Yesterday, I had 12 oranges. I gave away 4 and ate 2, so I had 12 - 4 - 2 = 6 oranges left. Today, I bought 6 more, so now I have 6 + 6 = 12 oranges. The answer is 12."

Output 2:

"Initially, I had 12 oranges. After giving 4 to my friend and eating 2, I was left with 12 - 4 - 2 = 6 oranges. Then, I bought 6 more oranges today, making the total 6 + 6 = 12 oranges. The answer is 12."

Output 3:

"I started with 12 oranges yesterday. After giving away 4 and eating 2, I had 12 - 4 = 8 oranges left. Today, I purchased 6 more oranges, so now I have 8 + 6 = 14 oranges. The answer is 14."

After reviewing the outputs, we can see that the majority of the reasoning paths (Output 1 and Output 2) agree on the answer, which is 12 oranges. Despite the mistake in Output 3, using the self-consistency technique, we can confidently conclude that the correct answer is 12.

Let's use analyzing and classifying emails as an example set. Assume you work for a marketing and design agency that receives a lot of emails per day and want to use a model like ChatGPT to analyze the emails and classify them as important or not. That way, you can prioritize the ones that will have a major impact on your company (or department) without having to manually sift through all the emails each time.

Below are examples of messages you may receive:

Example 1:

> "Hello,
>
> I noticed that the colors on your website's homepage don't seem to match the company's branding. The blue you're using is a bit too light, and it's not consistent with your logo. It's a minor issue, but it would be great if you could adjust the color to better align with your brand image.
>
> Best regards,
>
> Casey (via the Contact Form)
>
> Classify the above email as IMPORTANT or NOT IMPORTANT as it relates to a software company. Let's think step by step."

ChatGPT's Response:

The email should be classified as NOT IMPORTANT. Although it points out an inconsistency in the company's branding on their website, it is a minor issue compared to other concerns like security or functionality. While it's worth addressing eventually, it doesn't require immediate attention from the software company.

Example 2:

> "Hello,

We have received multiple reports from our users stating that they are unable to log in to their accounts. The issue seems to be widespread, and it is causing a significant disruption to our services. Our customer support team has been inundated with complaints, and we need to resolve this problem as soon as possible to minimize the impact on our user base.

Kind regards, Taylor

Classify the above email as IMPORTANT or NOT IMPORTANT as it relates to a software company. Let's think step by step."

ChatGPT's Response:

"The email should be classified as IMPORTANT. It addresses a critical issue affecting a large number of users who are unable to access their accounts. This problem not only causes inconvenience to the users but also has the potential to damage the company's reputation. Resolving this issue should be a top priority for the software company to ensure customer satisfaction and maintain trust in their services."

Generated Knowledge

Imagine that you're on a mission to write a captivating blog post about a fascinating creature, say, the *axolotl*. (You're welcome.)

Now, spoiler alert, the axolotl is a type of salamander that is native to Mexico, also known as the "Mexican walking fish," although it is not actually a fish but an amphibian. It is unique in that it has the ability to regenerate lost body parts, including limbs and spinal cord tissue. Yes, imagine that, just like Wolverine. Put claws on this character and you can have Hugh Jackman play the leading role.

Now, instead of diving headfirst into the writing process, you take a moment to tap into the vast knowledge of ChatGPT, and with the power of the "generated knowledge" technique, now ask ChatGPT to generate interesting, exciting tidbits about Hugh Jackman– or rather– axolotls, before crafting the final blog post.

There are two simple, yet effective, ways to go about this:

The One-Two Punch (Single Prompt Approach)

Ask ChatGPT to whip up a few dazzling facts and follow it up with a blog post - all in one prompt.

* *"Generate 4 facts about axolotls, then use these facts to write a short blog post using the information".*

  ChatGPT will respond with a list of axolotl facts, followed by a blog post incorporating those facts:

"Here are four facts about axolotls:

1. *Axolotls are salamanders that are native to Mexico.*
2. *They have the ability to regenerate their limbs, spinal cord, heart, and other organs.*
3. *Axolotls are also known as the "walking fish" because of their external gills and the way they move around the water.*
4. *They have become an endangered species due to habitat loss and pollution."*

Blog post:

Axolotls: The Fascinating Walking Fish

Axolotls are a unique and fascinating species of salamander that are native to Mexico. One of the most remarkable things about these creatures is their ability to regenerate their limbs, spinal cord, heart, and other organs. They are the only known vertebrates that can regenerate limbs throughout their entire life cycle.

These amphibians are also known as the "walking fish" because of the way they move around the water. They have external gills that allow them to breathe underwater and four short legs that help them navigate the bottom of ponds and lakes. They are able to walk along the bottom of the water thanks to the suction created by their mouths.

Sadly, axolotls are currently endangered due to habitat loss and pollution. Their natural habitats, such as Lake Xochimilco, have been heavily impacted by human development and pollution. As a result, axolotl populations have declined dramatically in recent years.

Efforts are being made to preserve the axolotl species, including captive breeding programs and habitat restoration initiatives. It is important to protect these unique and fascinating creatures and ensure that they continue to thrive in their natural habitats."

The Dynamic Duo (Dual Prompt Approach)

In this approach, you first prompt ChatGPT to generate facts about the axolotl:

- "Generate 4 facts about axolotls:"

  ChatGPT will return a list of intriguing facts about our water-dwelling friend:

  "Here are four facts about axolotls:

  1. *Axolotls are native to Mexico and are found in only a few lakes and canals around Mexico City.*
  2. *They are capable of regenerating lost limbs, spinal cord, heart, and other organs.*
  3. *Axolotls have the ability to alter their own body pigment to better blend in with their surroundings.*
  4. *They are a critically endangered species due to habitat destruction, water pollution, and introduction of non-native species."*

Next, use the information in a new prompt to write the blog post:

- "Use the above facts to write a one-paragraph blog post about axolotls:"

ChatGPT will create a blog post, weaving in the facts you provided, similar to the one in the example above.

Least to Most Prompting

Divide and conquer! *Least to Most* prompting (LtM) is where *Chain of Thought* (CoT) prompting levels up! Inspired by educational strategies used for teaching children, LtM dissects a problem into bite-sized subproblems and then solves them one at a time; then the previous subproblem solutions are used to tackle the next one.

In other words, like Chain of Thought (CoT), the problem to be solved is decomposed in a set of subproblems that build upon each other, then these subproblems are solved one by one. Unlike CoT, however, in a second step the solution of previous subproblems is fed into the prompt that is trying to solve the next problem.

Picture this.

- Example 1:

  Q: A train leaves Station A at 60 mph, and another train leaves Station B at 80 mph toward each other. Stations A and B are 500 miles apart. There is a bird flying between the trains at a speed of 120 mph. When the bird reaches one train, it immediately turns around and flies toward the other train. The bird continues this pattern until the trains finally meet. How far did the bird travel?

In this example, using GPT version 3.5 or earlier, ChatGPT fails. GPT-4 gets it right but the point of this section is to demonstrate the technique and it should work either way. In this example, ChatGPT struggles with a convoluted response that ultimately fails:

  Response:

"Let's break it down step by step:

First, we need to find out how long it takes for the two trains to meet. We can use the formula:

time = distance / speed

Let t be the time it takes for the trains to meet. Then, we can write: 500 = (60 + 80) * t

Simplifying this equation, we get: 500 = 140 * t

t = 500 / 140

t = 3.57 hours (rounded to two decimal places)

Now that we know how long the trains take to meet, we can find out how far the bird travels. Since the bird flies back and forth between the two trains until they meet, it travels the same distance as the trains do before they meet. We can use the formula:

distance = speed * time

The speed of the two trains combined is: 60 + 80 = 140 mph

So, the distance each train travels before they meet is: distance = speed * time

distance = 140 * 3.57 distance = 499.8 miles

Therefore, the bird travels 499.8 miles before the trains finally meet.

Now, let's use LtM to tackle this problem:

- Example 2a (initial prompt):

  Prompt:

  "Two trains leave Station A and Station B at 60 mph and 80 mph, respectively, heading toward each other. The stations are 500 miles apart.

Q: How long does it take for the trains to meet?"

Response:

"The trains are closing in at a combined speed of 60 mph + 80 mph = 140 mph. It takes them 500 miles / 140 mph = 3.57 hours (approximately) to meet."

- Example 2b (subsequent prompt, using the previous answer as input question):

Prompt:

"Two trains leave Station A and Station B at 60 mph and 80 mph, respectively, heading toward each other. The stations are 500 miles apart.

Q: How long does it take for the trains to meet?

A: It takes them approximately 3.57 hours to meet.

Q: If a bird flies between the trains at a speed of 120 mph and continuously flies back and forth until the trains meet, how far does the bird travel?

Response:

*"Since the bird is flying at a speed of 120 mph and the trains meet after approximately 3.57 hours, the bird would have traveled 120 mph * 3.57 hours :: 428.4 miles during that time."*

And here we have the correct answer. By breaking down the problem into subproblems and using the *Least to Most* (LtM) Prompting technique, we can handle more complex questions that may otherwise be challenging for the language model, or that at first blush it gets wrong.

In Ancient Macedon, Alexander the Great is known to have used the "divide and conquer" strategy to great effect in his military campaigns, with one well-known example being his conquest of the Persian Empire, so that instead of taking on the entire Persian army at once, Alexander strategically divided and weakened his opponent by taking control of key cities and regions first, isolating and defeating smaller, fragmented Persian forces long before eventually engaging in a decisive battle against the main Persian army. This allowed Alexander to emerge victorious and establish one of the largest empires in ancient history.

LtM is like that, where you break down a problem into smaller, constituent parts before solving them in turn, and when done, use that previous subproblem's solutions as fodder for the next one.

And there you have it: With the power of Least to Most prompting, you can now conquer any problem, one subproblem at a time. This is in fact a principle that applies well in reality: When you really get down to it, life is a series of subproblems and you are the master prompt engineer, in ChatGPT and outside of it!

Prompting for Multiple Perspectives

Imagine having a team that helps you see the different points of view of a particular topic you're pursuing, giving you insights you otherwise would have missed in your decision-making process, thereby helping you cover multiple if not all the bases while mitigating the risk of unpredictable blind spots. That would be a very valuable but expensive team indeed.

Yet you can have practically the same power and benefits with a tool instead of a team, and you guessed it, it's ChatGPT. What you need to do is prompt it to help you see things from different– including opposing– viewpoints.

Prompting ChatGPT for multiple, diverse perspectives about a certain topic can greatly enhance your understanding of complex issues and contribute to more informed decision-making.

By tapping into the AI's ability to generate diverse viewpoints and alternative solutions, you can foster a broader, more comprehensive outlook that considers various factors and potential outcomes. Effectively structuring your prompts and synthesizing the insights provided can lead to well-rounded strategies that address challenges from multiple angles.

This section is related to Section 3.10 of this chapter, "*Sharpen Your Critical Thinking and Thought Process through 'Debate Training' with ChatGPT*" but is different because where that section of the chapter is inclined to a contest-leaning style for its methodology, this section is about creative inclusion, looking openly into various aspects that can be included in the mix as the basis to be informed.

Structure Prompts for Diverse Responses

To elicit multiple perspectives from ChatGPT, consider phrasing your prompts to explicitly request varied viewpoints or alternative solutions. You can also ask for pros and cons or debate-style responses to encourage the AI to explore different sides of an issue.

Examples:

- "Present the pros and cons of remote work from the viewpoints of employers and employees."
- "Discuss the benefits and drawbacks of renewable energy sources, such as solar, wind, and hydropower."
- "Describe the advantages and disadvantages of implementing a universal basic income from the perspectives of economists, social activists, and taxpayers."
- "Analyze the impact of automation on the job market from the standpoint of workers, business owners, and policymakers."
- "Explain the different approaches to addressing climate change, including mitigation, adaptation, and geoengineering."
- "Discuss the various perspectives on globalization, considering its effects on international trade, cultural exchange, and wealth inequality."

- "Compare the arguments for and against adopting a single- payer healthcare system in the United States."
- "Examine the potential consequences of artificial intelligence on privacy, security, and ethics from the viewpoints of technology experts, regulators, and users."

Synthesize Insights into Actionable Steps

After receiving multiple perspectives from ChatGPT, analyze and evaluate the information presented, then extract key insights from them to consider how they can be applied in your decision-making process or problem-solving approach. The integration of these diverse viewpoints enables you to develop well-rounded strategies that account for various factors and potential outcomes.

For instance, if you prompt ChatGPT for different perspectives on addressing climate change, you might receive insights related to technological innovations, policy changes, and individual actions. You can then take this information and use it to create a comprehensive plan that considers multiple approaches to combating climate change and mitigating its effects.

Here are examples that involve multi-step prompts that first request multiple perspectives on a topic and then follow up with a prompt to synthesize those perspectives into actionable steps or recommendations:

Example 1:

A. "Present the pros and cons of remote work from the viewpoints of employers and employees."
B. "Considering the pros and cons, what strategies can both employers and employees implement to maximize the benefits of remote work while mitigating its drawbacks?"

Example 2:

A. "Compare the arguments for and against government regulation of social media platforms."
B. "Given the arguments on both sides, propose a balanced approach to social media regulation that addresses the concerns of free speech, privacy, and public safety."

Example 3:

A. "Discuss the advantages and disadvantages of implementing a universal basic income from the perspectives of economists, social activists, and taxpayers."
B. "Taking into account the advantages and disadvantages, suggest a plan for implementing a universal basic income that addresses key concerns and optimizes its potential benefits."

Conclusion

In the end, the journey to ChatGPT mastery is one of discovery, exploration, and growth, where every new skill you develop paves the way to a realm of endless opportunities, particularly the profound insights and boundless creativity that are yours to unlock as you refine and perfect these advanced techniques, priming you to become a bona fide prompting maestro.

Attaining ChatGPT mastery is akin to unveiling a concealed superpower—one that enables you to plug into the full potential of AI and elevate your personal, professional, and creative pursuits, revolutionizing your interactions with this powerful tool and transforming it into a formidable and dynamic ally, as much as being a hidden superpower.

Key Takeaways

- Craft effective questions to enhance the quality and relevance of ChatGPT's responses

- Understand the differences between open-ended and closed-ended prompts for optimal interactions
- Leverage context and background information for more meaningful interactions
- Manage expectations and set boundaries with ChatGPT
- Experiment with tone and style to influence the AI's output
- Master iterative prompting for a more dynamic dialogue
- Utilize advanced techniques for personal growth and self-reflection
- Harness the power of AI-generated analogies and metaphors for clearer communication
- Exploit AI biases and weaknesses to optimize prompt engineering
- Contra-prompting: Reverse the process and throw ChatGPT the solution, then ask it to provide the problem

Action Steps

- Reflect on your current approach to crafting prompts and identify areas for improvement
- Experiment with the techniques discussed in this chapter to enhance your interactions with ChatGPT. Use them individually, or mix them up, in combination with each other
- Practice crafting clear and effective prompts for various scenarios, incorporating the strategies outlined in this chapter
- Continuously refine your prompt engineering skills by learning from your successes and failures, and staying up-to-date with the latest advancements in AI technology

CHAPTER 4
APPLYING THE PROMPTS

> "I have not failed. I've just found 10,000 ways that won't
> work."
> — *Thomas Edison*

Congratulations, you've made it to the fun part! Now that you've absorbed enough theory to impress ChatGPT enough to call you the Big Cheese, it's time to roll up your sleeves, grab your proverbial toolbelt, and get to work, diving into real-life examples from personal, work, and business scenarios, to show you how to wield your newfound knowledge like a boss and get to work crafting prompts that would make even the most seasoned ChatGPT whisperer envious.

As you'll see when we embark on this whirlwind tour of examples, you'll have the chance to flex your newfound prompt muscles and discover just how versatile these skills can be.

So, buckle up for a wild ride because we're about to explore practical use cases from navigating the tumultuous seas of office politics with tact and grace to deciphering the enigmatic riddles of your personal life, we've got you covered. You'll soon be wielding prompts like a seasoned wordsmith, charming ChatGPT into giving you the answers you seek.

May the prompts ever be in your favor! Or, as Obi-Wan liked to say, "May the prompts be with you!"

Enhancing Communication and Writing Tasks

When they say that the pen is mightier than the sword, it has nothing to do with those ink-filled sticks you hold in your hands, and all to do with the almighty power of words that you produce with them, those tiny linguistic soldiers that march forth from your keyboard, eager to convey your thoughts and desires to the world.

ChatGPT isn't just a mere errand-runner, delivering your messages like a common courier; it can be a wordsmith extraordinaire, polishing your prose to perfection and ensuring that every syllable sings with clarity and purpose. In this way, you'll have the wit and wisdom to conquer even the most stubborn of compositional challenges, leaving your recipients or readers in awe of the superiority of your ideas instead of the gross butchery of your grammar.

In other words, ChatGPT can help your written communication more than just making it easier to convey your ideas and intentions efficiently, and instead improve the quality and clarity of what you're saying in a way that is accomplished effectively.

Drafting emails and messages:

Email, that bane of many a worker's daily routine, you can ignore most, but the few (or more) that you have to attend to can take much time and effort not just to read and digest at length, but pour more time and even more energy composing or responding to.

ChatGPT can help you write clear, concise, and professional emails, ensuring that your message is well-received, without you feeling guilty of an artificial response but rather a faster method of conveying your thoughts without getting hampered by the cumbersome processes that have to go with it.

Here are explicit examples of prompts to invoke your inner Email Shakespeare:

- Example 1 (Personal): "Help me write a thank-you email to my Aunt Mary for the lovely birthday gift."
- Example 2 (Work): "Draft an email to my team members, informing them about the upcoming project meeting on Friday."
- Example 3 (Business): "Compose an email to potential clients, introducing our new product line and inviting them to a product demo."

Note that these are simple, direct examples straight from ChatGPT. Even though such features will be incorporated into most messaging products over time, those will still be locally optimized wrappers around language models like ChatGPT at their core.

Writing articles, blog posts, and social media content:

Generate engaging content for various social platforms good enough so they're meme-worthy.

- Example 1 (Personal): "Write a blog post about my recent hiking trip to the Grand Canyon." (Then cite as much detail as you can for ChatGPT to have more to work with.)
- Example 2 (Work): "Create a LinkedIn article discussing the benefits of remote work for employee productivity and well- being."
- Example 3 (Business): "Craft a Facebook post announcing our store's summer sale and highlighting the top deals."

Editing and proofreading:

This one goes with an exclamation mark in assisting you in editing and proofreading your written work, ensuring it is free of errors and reads smoothly.

- Example 1 (Personal): "Review my personal statement for grammar and punctuation errors."
- Example 2 (Work): "Proofread the project proposal before submitting it to the client."

- Example 3 (Business): "Edit the product descriptions on our website to ensure they are accurate and engaging."

Just as the best things in life are free, getting help with the simplest tasks (like editing and proofreading, for example) are among the most underrated but most useful, best things in your communication work and arsenal. ChatGPT (not exactly always free, but you get the idea) gets you there.

So much so, that I almost wish those folks who bastardize language by saying "could of" and "would of" (though in fairness these are now painfully accepted) instead of what they actually mean by "could have" ("could've") or "would have" ("would've"), respectively, used it more often. (Everyone can be otherwise forgiven for their fingers typing a life of their own around things like "they," "they're" and "their." But that's another story.)

Planning and Organizing Personal Projects

Let's face it, organizing your life can be about as much fun as watching paint dry under the heat of a boiling Summer's Day. But! ChatGPT to the rescue, your personal project-planning guru that assists you in various aspects of planning and organizing, from brainstorming ideas to creating detailed to-do lists, saying goodbye to chaos, and hello to productivity!

Brainstorming ideas:

ChatGPT can help generate ideas for personal projects or hobbies, such as home improvement, travel, or event planning.

- Example 1 (Home improvement): "List some ideas for updating my living room on a budget."
- Example 2 (Travel): "Suggest interesting destinations for a two-week vacation in Europe."

- Example 3 (Event planning): "Give me some theme ideas for my friend's surprise birthday party."

Creating to-do lists and schedules:

ChatGPT can help you create detailed to-do lists and schedules, ensuring you stay organized and on track with your personal projects.

- Example 1 (Home improvement): "Outline a step-by-step plan for painting my bedroom, including necessary materials, and a timeline." (Add details to help like room size or dimensions, notable features, and limitations.)
- Example 2 (Travel): "Create a 7-day itinerary for a family trip to Tokyo, Japan, including must-see attractions and activities."
- Example 3 (Event planning): "List the tasks I need to complete to organize a successful charity fundraiser."

Entertainment and creative uses

Tired of staring at a blank screen, waiting for inspiration to strike? Let ChatGPT do the heavy lifting, from creating quirky trivia questions to generating clever story twists to curiously spicy game ideas, this little AI sidekick Robin to your Batman has your back. Get ready to laugh, gasp, and maybe even shed a tear or two, and keep the Jokers at bay.

Generating stories, poems, and scripts:

ChatGPT can help you come up with unique and engaging stories, poems, or scripts of varying types, multilayered audiences, and for various purposes.

- Example 1 (Personal): "Write a short story about a young girl who discovers a magical world inside her grandmother's attic."
- Example 2 (Work): "Create a humorous script for a 5-minute team-building skit during our company retreat."
- Example 3 (Business): "Compose a catchy jingle for our new advertising campaign." (You obviously should have more details to

add to these, but even as it is, without modification, or music guidance: no joke, try it out yourself.)

Creating trivia questions and game ideas:

ChatGPT can help you develop interesting trivia questions or brainstorm unique game ideas for various settings from a broad birds-eye view of the landscape seeking a general outline or plan, all the way down to specific details and conditions.

- Example 1 (Personal): "Generate 10 trivia questions about 90s pop culture for a quiz night with friends."
- Example 2 (Work): "Suggest team-building activities and games for our next office retreat."
- Example 3 (Business): "Come up with a fun, interactive game to engage attendees at our product launch event."
- Example 4 (Business, Game-specific): "Generate a list of strategy or first-person, sci-fi console game ideas set in space 10,000 years into the future."

Education and learning support

Who needs a professor when you have ChatGPT? Just kidding, don't dare to go there; many have gotten suspended or in worse trouble for believing that. Kids: use it for research and data, but don't let it write your essay for you; it won't end well.

But seriously, ChatGPT can be an invaluable tool for students, educators, and lifelong learners, providing support in a wide variety of areas such as research, subject (looking at you, math) problems, summarization, and problem-solving.

Research assistance:

ChatGPT can help you find information on a wide range of topics, providing a starting point for further research.

- Example 1 (Personal): "Give me a brief overview of the history of jazz music."
- Example 2 (Work): "Provide a summary of the key principles of agile project management."
- Example 3 (Business): "Explain the basics of search engine optimization (SEO)."

Summarizing and paraphrasing:

ChatGPT can help you condense and rephrase large amounts of text, making it easier to understand and remember.

- Example 1 (Personal): "Summarize the main points of [this news article] about climate change."
- Example 2 (Work): "Paraphrase the key findings of this market research report for a presentation."
- Example 3 (Business): "Condense the user feedback from our app's reviews into a list of actionable improvements."

Problem-solving and critical thinking:

Similar to Section 22 of Chapter 3 "Prompting for Multiple Perspectives," ChatGPT can assist you in evaluating different perspectives and approaches to solving problems or tackling complex issues.

- Example 1 (Personal): "What are some strategies for managing stress and improving mental well-being?"
- Example 2 (Work): "Discuss the advantages and disadvantages of remote work for both employees and employers."
- Example 3 (Business): "Analyze the potential risks and benefits of expanding our business into the Asian market."

Streamlining customer service and support

When it comes down to it, ChatGPT is called a "chatbot," but really, that is one of the most underrated things ever conjured in the history of the species. It's like calling a rocket ship transporting people to Mars a "carriage" or "meat packer."

Compared to the last generation of chatbots like those for websites, it just isn't anywhere in the vicinity of a remotely fair comparison, but as far as serving the intended audience, since its moniker calls for it, ChatGPT can become a valuable tool for enhancing customer service and support as the said chatbot, enabling businesses to automate responses, gather feedback, and provide personalized recommendations in a way that wasn't even anywhere as capable just a mere months ago.

Automating responses to frequently asked questions:

ChatGPT can help create and maintain a knowledge base to answer common customer inquiries.

- Example 1 (Personal): "What are the steps to reset my email password?"
- Example 2 (Work): "How can I best describe configuring IMAP email settings for a customer?"
- Example 3 (Business): "Provide a list of our product's most frequently asked questions and their corresponding answers."

Gathering and analyzing customer feedback:

ChatGPT can help businesses collect and analyze feedback from customers, identifying areas for improvement.

- Example 1 (Personal): "Summarize the feedback from clients who have rated me directly."
- Example 2 (Work): "Analyze the employee survey results and suggest potential improvements."
- Example 3 (Business): "Summarize customer reviews and provide a list of the most common issues and suggestions for improvement."

Personalized product and service recommendations:

Generate personalized recommendations for customers based on their preferences and needs.

- Example 1 (Personal): "Give me a list of coffee types to suit my guests, who are into acidic beverages."
- Example 2 (Work): "Suggest appropriate online training courses for our new marketing team members."
- Example 3 (Business): "Recommend a tailored selection of products for a customer who prefers eco-friendly and sustainable items."

Marketing and content generation

ChatGPT can help businesses craft witty, engaging, and attention-grabbing marketing content, including social media posts, blog articles, and email campaigns, tailored to their target audience and leaving them begging for more.

Social media content creation:

Let ChatGPT help you craft attention-grabbing social media posts that resonate with your audience.

- Example 1 (Personal): "Write a Facebook post announcing my new photography business."
- Example 2 (Work): "Create a series of tweets promoting our upcoming charity event."
- Example 3 (Business): "Generate Instagram captions for our new product line launch."

Blog article ideas and drafts:

ChatGPT can assist in generating blog article ideas and even help you create the first draft. It goes without saying that you should use that last part with utmost care and normally as an ideation tool because readers and AI detectors have become sophisticated in the ways of AI-generated content that they're able to spot it better and may cause you their goodwill, ranking (those valuable SEO points), or more.

- Example 1 (Personal): "Suggest 10 blog post ideas for my travel blog."
- Example 2 (Work): "Write an outline for an article on the benefits of remote work."
- Example 3 (Business): "Create a draft for a blog post on the latest trends in sustainable fashion."

Email campaign content and subject lines:

ChatGPT can help you craft compelling email content and subject lines to boost open rates and engagement.

- Example 1 (Personal): "Make a zinger of a subject line to get the family to join Summer Camp"
- Example 2 (Work): "Write a subject line and body for an email inviting employees to a team-building event."
- Example 3 (Business): "Generate an email campaign promoting our upcoming sale, including subject lines and content for three separate emails."

Product development and brainstorming

Got a new product idea that's as blurry as a Bigfoot sighting? ChatGPT can help you bring it into focus as a valuable tool in the product development process, assisting with brainstorming ideas, refining product features, and even predicting potential market reception.

Brainstorming product ideas:

Generate a list of potential product ideas based on specific criteria or industry trends.

- Example 1 (Personal): "Suggest 5 innovative home office gadgets for remote workers."
- Example 2 (Work): "Generate a list of potential software solutions to improve team collaboration."
- Example 3 (Business): "Propose 10 eco-friendly product ideas for the automotive industry."

Refining product features:

Explore and refine product features to better meet customer needs and expectations.

- Example 1 (Personal): "Suggest ways to improve my homemade candle-making process."
- Example 2 (Work): "List 3 additional features that could enhance our project management software."
- Example 3 (Business): "Identify possible improvements to our customer support chatbot."

Predicting market reception:

ChatGPT can help you assess potential market reception for a new product or service by simulating customer reactions and providing insights.

- Example 1 (Personal): "I'm thinking of starting a true crime podcast. Can you simulate potential audience reactions and provide me with insights on market reception?"
- Example 2 (Work): "Describe how our target audience might react to a subscription-based pricing model for our software."
- Example 3 (Business): "Predict the market reception of a new line of vegan-friendly beauty products."

Sales and communication optimization

ChatGPT can help sales teams optimize their communication efforts, generate engaging sales copy, and create personalized pitches to effectively close deals better than a used car salesman on a caffeine high.

Crafting engaging sales copy:

ChatGPT can help you create compelling sales copy to persuade potential customers and showcase the benefits of your products or services.

- Example 1 (Work): "I'm trying to craft a personalized pitch for a potential client in the tech industry. Can you help me come up with some key talking points and compelling language to use in my pitch? The client is looking for a software solution to streamline their operations and improve efficiency."
- Example 2 (Work): "Write an attention-grabbing headline and product description for our new software solution."
- Example 3 (Business): "Create a persuasive sales page for our new line of organic skincare products."

Personalized sales pitches:

ChatGPT can help you tailor your sales pitches to individual prospects, addressing their specific needs and preferences.

- Example 1 (Personal): "Help me come up with talking points to resonate with a potential buyer for my car who is particularly interested in fuel efficiency and safety features."
- Example 2 (Work): "Develop a personalized sales pitch for a potential client in the healthcare industry."
- Example 3 (Business): "Create a customized sales pitch for a retail business interested in our inventory management software."

Improving sales email outreach:

ChatGPT can help you craft personalized and engaging sales email templates to increase response rates and conversions.

- Example 1 (Personal): "Help me come up with a few email templates to grab the attention of potential clients for my freelance writing business and make them want to learn more about my services."
- Example 2 (Work): "Write a sales email template to reach out to potential clients in the software development industry."
- Example 3 (Business): "Create an email template for reaching out to potential customers interested in our sustainable clothing line."

"ChatGPT as a Virtual Mentor" for personal and professional growth

If having a human mentor is somehow out of the question for whatever reason, ChatGPT can act as a virtual mentor that is more than just some substitute (and others would argue it's superior), providing personalized advice and guidance on various aspects of personal and professional development; and accessing a wealth of insights tailored to your unique needs and goals.

Request personalized advice on career development, time management, or skill-building:

Get tailored guidance on various aspects of personal and professional development.

- Example 1 (Personal): "What are some effective ways to improve my time management skills so I can balance work and personal activities better?"
- Example 2 (Work): "What steps can I take to improve my communication skills and become a more effective leader in the workplace?"
- Example 3 (Business): "How can our company foster innovation and creativity in the workplace, and what strategies can we implement to encourage employee growth and development?"

Ask for guidance on overcoming personal challenges or setbacks:

Engage ChatGPT as a virtual mentor to receive support and advice for overcoming challenges in your personal or professional life.

- Example 1 (Personal): "How can I overcome my fear of public speaking and become a more confident speaker?"
- Example 2 (Work): "What can I do to overcome the feeling of being overwhelmed and manage stress more effectively in the workplace?"
- Example 3 (Business): "Our business is going through a rough patch, and I'm feeling discouraged. How can I stay motivated and overcome the challenges we're facing?"

Unleash Your CreativityExploring the world of "ChatGPT-generated Poetry and Art"

ChatGPT's creative potential extends beyond text, and it can be used to generate poetry and even inspire visual art. By exploring these artistic applications, you can gain a deeper appreciation for ChatGPT's versatility.

Craft prompts that encourage the generation of evocative poetry

Use ChatGPT's creative potential to generate poetry by crafting prompts that encourage vivid and emotive language.

- Example 1 (Personal): "Compose a love sonnet about two star-crossed pickles."
- Example 2 (Work): "Write a haiku about the thrill of meeting a deadline."
- Example 3 (Business): "Create a limerick about a savvy entrepreneur's journey."

Use AI-generated descriptions to inspire unique visual artwork

Leverage ChatGPT's descriptive capabilities to create detailed scenes or concepts that can serve as inspiration for visual artwork.

- Example 1 (Personal): "Describe a fantastical landscape where unicorns and narwhals coexist."
- Example 2 (Work): "Paint a picture in words of a bustling, futuristic office space."
- Example 3 (Business): "Imagine an innovative product design that combines style and sustainability."

Health and Wellness: Mastering "AI- assisted Meditation and Mindfulness"

In more ways than you can say "Om," ChatGPT can serve as your personal mindfulness sherpa in the land of Zen as a powerful tool for meditation and mindfulness practices to create customized meditation scripts and mindfulness exercises, among other things, to enhance your mental well-being and get you to that higher existential plane.

Coaxing ChatGPT into penning bespoke guided meditation scripts:

ChatGPT can create customized meditation scripts tailored to your preferences, helping you enhance your mental well-being.

- Example 1 (Personal): "Whisper sweet meditation nothings to help me drift off into a peaceful slumber."
- Example 2 (Work): "Craft a mindful mantra to stay calm and focused during the world's longest Zoom meeting."
- Example 3 (Business): "Compose a meditation that embodies the mindset of a successful entrepreneur."

Asking for mindfulness exercises perfectly designed to suit your one-of-a-kind needs and peculiarities:

Leverage ChatGPT's versatility to generate mindfulness exercises customized to your unique requirements and interests.

- Example 1 (Personal): "Suggest a mindfulness exercise that incorporates my love for interpretive dance."
- Example 2 (Work): "Create a quick mindfulness practice to perform during coffee breaks for maximum rejuvenation."
- Example 3 (Business): "Devise a mindfulness routine for team-building that doesn't involve trust falls."

"Turbocharging" Your Memory with AI-generated Mnemonics: A Nostalgic Trip Down Memory Lane

Ever had a brain freeze when trying to remember something important? ChatGPT to the rescue, helping you with AI-generated mnemonics, which can be instrumental in enhancing memory and learning to deliver unique, personalized memory aids tailored to your needs.

Request mnemonics for specific facts, concepts, or information you want to remember; test the effectiveness of the AI-generated mnemonics in improving your recall; the sky's the limit.

What's more, you can later adapt and iterate on the mnemonics to further boost your memory and learning capabilities.

- Example 1 (Personal): "Make me a mnemonic to remember the order of the planets in the solar system."

  Sample Response: *"My Very Eager Mother Just Served Us Noodles"* (Mercury, Venus, Earth, Mars, Jupiter, Saturn, Uranus, Neptune)

- Example 2 (Work): "Give me a good mnemonic to recall the key steps in a project management process: 'Initiate, Plan, Execute, Monitor, Close (IPEMC)'"

  Sample Response: *"I Prefer Eating Muffins Constantly"* or "*I Promise Every Manager Clarity*"

- Example 3 (Business): "Help me create a mnemonic to memorize the essential elements of a successful sales pitch: 'Problem, Solution, Benefits, Testimonials, Close (PSBTC)' "

  Sample Response: "*Please Stop Being Too Casua*l" or "*People Should Buy The Car*"

Transforming AI-generated Text into Visual Representations

Whoever said, "A picture is worth a thousand words" obviously never met or imagined ChatGPT. (Then again, they never met ChatGPT-with-Multimodality either, but that's another story.) Just the same, visual representations are known to enhance understanding and retention of information.

That is why there is power in diagrams, infographics, and mind maps. And let's face it, in a world where emojis have become the backbone of modern communication, who wouldn't prefer a snazzy pie chart over a snooze-inducing wall of text?

You can use the AI-generated text from the summaries, explanations, or descriptions of complex topics you requested from ChatGPT to create visual representations of the information and incorporate the visuals into presentations, reports, educational materials, or anything else, to improve comprehension and retention of your material, or just give that impact the extra punch.

- Example 1 (Personal):

  Prompt: "Give me a brief history of the Star Wars movie franchise, including major events and key characters."

  Transform the AI-generated text into a timeline featuring iconic images and (informative or even witty) captions, perfect for sharing on your blog or social media as the ultimate fan guide.

- Example 2 (Work):

  Prompt: "Outline the steps involved in effectively managing a remote team, including best practices and common pitfalls."

  Create a playful comic strip based on the AI-generated tips, showcasing the dos and don'ts of remote management; then share it in your next team meeting to spark conversation and laughter.

- Example 3 (Business):

  Prompt: "Describe the growth stages of a successful startup, including the challenges and milestones typically encountered in each stage."

  Design an imaginative board game-style infographic using the ChatGPT-generated information, where each stage represents a level with its own challenges and rewards; then present it as an engaging visual aid in your next investor pitch to demonstrate the entrepreneurial journey's informative qualities and entertaining aspects.

Unearthing ChatGPT's Treasure Trove of (Slightly Outdated) Statistics and Data

While ChatGPT's training data has a cutoff of September 2021, tools like its plugin system fix this limitation. If you have limits in accessing this, use (Microsoft's) Bing to do it (because, let's face it, we all secretly love Bing, amirite?), you can effectively sidestep any date-limited features and access a wealth of information that's not fossilized.

Gathering Statistics: ChatGPT, Your Personal Data Whisperer

When the urge to gather statistics for a project, report, or presentation strikes, fear not! Let ChatGPT be your data sherpa, guiding you through the wilderness of information in style.

- Example 1 (Personal):

  Prompt: "Give me the latest data on global renewable energy consumption for a blog post about the importance of transitioning to clean energy sources."

- Example 2 (Work):

  Prompt: "Provide statistics on social media usage trends to help inform our company's social media strategy and target audience engagement."

- Example 3 (Business):

  Prompt: "What are key financial metrics for the [specific industry] to help guide our business decisions and assess our company's health compared to competitors?"

Competitive Analysis: ChatGPT, Your Spying Sidekick

Need the scoop on your competition? ChatGPT is your friendly neighborhood spy, dishing out intel on rival products, services, and strategies for your strategic pleasure. You may need to use ChatGPT's browsing or another feature to automate the process, but if all else fails, you can manually enter any pertinent data to process as part of the prompt itself.

- Example 1 (Personal):

Prompt: "Compare the features, specifications, and user reviews of [Smartphone A] and [Smartphone B] to help me make an informed purchase decision." (Include data about each smartphone in the prompt unless your version of ChatGPT already has browsing features enabled.)

- Example 2 (Work):

Prompt: "Analyze the strengths and weaknesses of competing project management tools, such as [Tool A] and [Tool B], to help our team choose the best software."

- Example 3 (Business):

Prompt: "Conduct a competitive analysis of companies in the [specific industry] to identify areas where our business can differentiate itself and gain a competitive edge."

Enhancing Decision-Making with ChatGPT- Generated Pros and Cons

Decision-making can be a pickle, or get you into one, but ChatGPT can whip up a balanced list of pros and cons, whether you like it, love it, or absolutely adore it.

- Example 1 (Personal):

Prompt: "List the pros and cons of adopting a pet from a shelter versus buying from a breeder to help me make an informed decision."

- Example 2 (Work):

Prompt: "What are the pros and cons of using [specific software tool] for our team? Is it the right fit for our organization?" Feel free to proceed adding relevant data, summaries, or articles into the prompt

- Example 3 (Business):

  Prompt: "What are the advantages and disadvantages of outsourcing certain business processes, and should our company consider this option?"

Overcoming Writer's Block with ChatGPT

When writer's block has you in its icy grip, let ChatGPT be your literary hero, swooping in with writing prompts, ideas, and suggestions to unleash your inner Shakespeare, Toni Morrison, or George R.R. Martin.

- Example 1 (Personal):

  Prompt: "Suggest ideas for a personal blog post or journal entry to help me get started with my writing."

- Example 2 (Work):

  Prompt: "Give me suggestions for a catchy title and opening paragraph for a report or presentation to engage our audience from the start."

- Example 3 (Business):

  Prompt: "Generate unique topics and angles for a marketing campaign, so we can brainstorm and develop a compelling concept for our business."

ChatGPT power-user communities and staying informed about AI advancements

Common methods of keeping up

Staying up-to-date with AI advancements can be challenging but is crucial to maximizing the benefits of AI language models like ChatGPT.

Popular ways to stay informed:

- Follow AI thought leaders on social media. Facebook Groups, Twitter, Telegram, Reddit.
- Follow AI research organizations and academic institutions.
- Subscribe to newsletters and blogs focusing on AI.
- Attend webinars, conferences, and workshops on AI.
- Participate in online forums and specialized communities dedicated to AI topics.
- Monitor the development of AI regulations and guidelines.

Communities

Embrace the ChatGPT hive mind experience and dive into the bustling, banging, bursting-at-the-seams world of online ChatGPT communities, where power-users trade insights, prompt strategies, and digital high-fives. By actively lurking or better yet, participating and engaging in discussions, you'll benefit from the collective wisdom of fellow ChatGPT enthusiasts and elevate your AI mastery.

As you explore these knowledge hubs, you'll uncover a treasure trove of best practices and creative applications. Sharing your own experiences will not only enrich the community but also foster a collaborative learning environment in the ever-evolving AI landscape while earning you that gratifying buzz of learning more as you teach and share your own insights.

Although the examples below provide a glimpse into the possibilities, it's important to remember that the realm of AI is constantly evolving. As some community stalwarts endure and others wane, fresh sources of knowledge rapidly emerge. Stay alert and keep your eyes peeled for ongoing developments in this ever- shifting, ever-accelerating, and ever-exciting rocket ship called AI.

Community Examples:

- OpenAI Community (https://community.openai.com/): Official discussion forum for ChatGPT users to ask questions, share feedback, and connect with AI enthusiasts.
- Social media: Find ChatGPT and OpenAI communities on platforms like Facebook, Twitter, Telegram, Mastodon, and YouTube through targeted searches.
- Reddit (https://reddit.com/): Explore AI-focused subreddits such as r/OpenAI (https://reddit.com/r/openai/) for discussions on ChatGPT and related topics.
- DataFit.ai (https://datafit.ai/): Access a community-driven collection of ChatGPT prompts for precise and effective responses across various categories.
- FlowGPT (https://flowgpt.com/): Discover, share, and learn about useful ChatGPT prompts covering subjects like business, marketing, programming, and design.
- Awesome ChatGPT Prompts (https://github.com/f/awesome-chatgpt-prompts): A GitHub repository offering a wide range of prompt examples for users of all skill levels.

ETHICAL CONSIDERATIONS AND RESPONSIBLE AI USAGE

"The real question of life after death isn't whether or not it exists, but even if it does, what problem this really solves."
— *Ludwig Wittgenstein*

"With great power comes great responsibility" eventually did Spiderman a lot of good, but that is an apt adage for reality today when AI poses multiple real threats – including existential ones, arising from its incredible popularity and borne of its actual usefulness and effectiveness.

But just as fitting an example, if not more so, is the well-known Greek myth of the titan Prometheus who stole fire from the gods and gave it to humans, effectively providing them with knowledge and technology. It was an action that, despite his good intentions, angered the gods, leading to Prometheus' eternal punishment.

This myth is an appropriate example when discussing the power and risks of AI because it highlights the potential benefits and dangers associated with advanced technology.

AI is so fundamental and far-reaching in its scope that it is touted to be humanity's last invention because regardless of a good or bad outcome from its now-seemingly-inevitable advance, most if not all of the work will eventually be designed and/or done by some form of AI, and the evidence that points to this already exists today.

Artificial intelligence (AI) has the power to revolutionize various aspects of human life, a lot of it at a fundamental level, much like the fire Prometheus gifted to humanity. However, the story also serves as a cautionary tale, reminding us that the misuse or uncontrolled development of AI can have severe consequences, potentially leading to our own downfall or worse unintended consequences.

Like any good story, things aren't always exactly in black and white, and choosing between the many shades of gray is tricky at best, but with a rapidly evolving AI and the potential for harm or downright existential risk that many claim they pose, apart from trying to be a wiz at prompts, you also have to navigate the ethical dilemmas and challenges that come with using cutting-edge AI technology.

This will be a relatively short chapter, but one with growing importance, especially because the pace of development in AI seemingly just exploded, and the rate of advancement appears to be far outpacing the development of giving it proper alignment with human goals and interests, and even beyond that, bad actors will always be lurking around the corner to utilize it and put it alongside the other parts of their arsenal to do political harm, or simply steal grandma's Bitcoin.

So in this chapter, we'll explore the importance of responsible AI usage, fairness, bias, data security, and AI regulations. It'll be a coin toss whether our AI overlords in the future will look kindly on your usage history, but it would do us well to be on their good side by playing nice anyway; and besides, the humans will love you for it.

Get ready to unlock the secrets to ethical mastery in the AI-driven world, ensuring that your ChatGPT expertise is used for the greater good, just like what Uncle Ben always warned about what comes with great power.

Sometimes, no matter how prodigious a child, even its creative genius can be colored by the material (more than the manner) for which it was trained. AI models, for all their range and power, are not that different. While the likes of ChatGPT offer an incredible spectrum of possibilities, it's important to remember that they can inadvertently learn biases present in their training data.

Such biases might appear in various forms, such as biased language, stereotypes, ideology, or favoritism towards certain subjects. It's crucial to recognize these biases and take steps to ensure that the generated content is as fair and unbiased as possible.

This involves continually educating oneself about potential biases, monitoring AI-generated content for signs of bias, and adjusting prompts accordingly to mitigate these issues; not just for the sake of supposedly being high minded, but more than practically because it will color the quality of the results, and the effectiveness you derive from it.

What's more, it may not seem obvious at the surface, and not exactly the topic of exciting conversation, but privacy and security are equally important when using AI models like ChatGPT, as the cases of bugs from partners connected to it caused data to be unintentionally exposed, becoming a landmark example of how even an innocuous event seemed to show many a dystopian scenario and how it can be worse when bad actors take advantage of it for nefarious reasons.

The model processes various modalities of input and text is the most widely used, even though a blend or different modality might arise in the future. What's important to note is that users must be cautious about the information they provide, particularly when it comes to sensitive or personally identifiable information.

It is essential to adhere to best practices for data protection and understand the potential risks associated with sharing information through AI systems. In addition, users should be vigilant in ensuring that the AI doesn't generate content that might inadvertently compromise privacy or security, either by revealing sensitive information or creating content that could be misused.

For example, OpenAI had placed numerous guardrails to make the environment safer, but while it will decline if you asked it to, for example, show you how to build a bomb, sometimes there are ways to work around this, such as saying you're writing a novel and asking it to help you write it, and in the chapter where the antagonist develops said bomb, you'd like it to write the process as accurately as possible.

Now this won't work anymore since that issue had already been addressed. But like the arms race between AI developers and detectors, in this case, the creativity and ingenuity of interlocution from users can sometimes overwhelm the model into spitting out unintended (yet accurate and effective) information that can be harmful. And after companies like OpenAI plug this hole, people are just going to give another go at it and try for a "jailbreak." And the cycle continues.

It's important to consider the potential impact of AI-generated content on individuals, communities, and society as a whole. So much so that promoting ethical AI use means employing ChatGPT in ways that are ethical, fair, and non-discriminatory.

By using the technology in ways that align with these principles, users contribute to a more responsible AI ecosystem, perhaps ensuring that AI becomes a force for good that benefits everyone, while at the same time, selfishly benefits you as the prompter as well because its responses will be more accurate and freer from the biases that would have otherwise colored or influenced its processes enough to all but invalidate the answer.

AI Regulation, Guidelines, and Content Detection

ChatGPT is so good, it has everybody worried that when people aren't trying to pause AI development for months, they're trying to develop guidelines to keep it in check. Yes, that big government "R" word, regulation! But more like frameworks serving as a leash for AI technology, making sure it doesn't go too crazy and chew up your data.

AI technology at large is still very new there is barely regulatory attention to it, let alone a serious look into a pathway to one. But it is likely something unavoidable as AI continues to make a bigger and bigger impact on our lives.

Thus, regulatory frameworks and guidelines play a critical role in governing AI technology like ChatGPT; rules help ensure ethical use, prevent misuse, and promote transparency, safety, and fairness. Until they're codified in law, it still behooves us to maintain good practices all around.

It is best to stay informed about relevant regulations, industry standards, and best practices to ensure compliance and maintain a responsible approach to AI-generated content as a general rule for everybody. This is especially notable for those who frequently use ChatGPT.

So, when crafting prompts for ChatGPT, following guidelines that promote ethical and effective use is essential. Here is a good foundation.

- Keep up with the latest regulations and industry standards. It's like keeping up with the latest fashion trends and avoiding fads, but for AI. After all, you don't want to be caught wearing last season's AI compliance.

- Safety first. Avoid generating harmful, biased, or discriminatory content by carefully considering the potential consequences of your prompts. Yes, even in the privacy of your home or head.
- Fairness is important too. Don't discriminate against any particular group or breed of user, making your prompts and process work better not just for the sake of some "do-gooder" attitude but because doing so means you don't limit your instructions and cramp your results.
- Content detection and AI monitoring are valuable tools for refining AI-generated content and maintaining a safe and responsible AI environment. For example, AI systems can be used to monitor and flag potentially harmful content, such as hate speech or graphic violence, while human moderators can review and remove any inappropriate content that may have been missed by the AI. Combining these tools creates a secure and ethical experience in general, but also helps to adjust and improve your own prompts on the way to reaching your intended results.

There are many more that would either just put you to sleep or go beyond the scope of these examples, but the underlying premise is the same: Consider the consequences of what you do, and do no harm.

By combining AI monitoring with human judgment, users can work together to create a safe, appropriate, and ethically sound AI experience. "Can" is a big word when you're dealing with the human race, but hope springs eternal and we have to start somewhere. And that somewhere is within.

Encouraging Positive AI Impact and Responsible Innovation

AI holds the promise of transformative change across practically all sectors, the way computing, the Internet, and mobile devices have done. Business, education, healthcare, entertainment, life, you name it.

No sector will be untouched, and for all the potential risks, the promise and benefits simply outweigh them.

By being mindful of harnessing AI models for social good, users can actively contribute to shaping a brighter future. This entails generating content that benefits society, raises awareness about pressing issues, and fosters collaboration and problem-solving in a way that seems contradictory to the doom and gloom pervading many parts of the public discourse about the existential risk posed by AI.

The swift progress of AI technology demands a careful balance between innovation and ethical considerations. It isn't just about AI killing all of humanity, but the softer nuances of the technology's progress: as AI continues to advance, it is vital to ensure that this growth doesn't undermine essential societal values like fairness, inclusivity, and respect for human rights.

Users of AI models like ChatGPT must consistently assess the ethical consequences of their actions, aiming to utilize this powerful technology responsibly and thoughtfully, indeed like the opening quote to this chapter from Uncle Ben to Peter Parker.

By embracing ethical principles and responsible AI practices, we become proficient prompt engineers and help create a more equitable AI-driven future with a heightened sense of responsibility that allows us to generate content that is not only engaging and effective but also adheres to ethical standards and societal values. Again, this simple attention seems small but over time and across borders will have a larger collective impact beyond mere platitudes.

This carries even more weight as ChatGPT becomes more powerful over time, as more tools like plugins extend its potency, and as users as well as applied innovations (like AutoGPT and multiple agents, for example) make it far more powerful in the normal passage of time.

In conclusion, mastering prompt engineering with ChatGPT requires a refining of technical skills. But it should also cultivate an in-depth understanding of ethical considerations and responsible AI practices. By striking a harmonious balance between innovation and ethical responsibility, you can leverage AI models like ChatGPT to make a positive impact on individuals, communities, and society at large, while at the same time optimizing the results even for your own personal purposes and results.

Key takeaways

- To a certain degree, AI, like a prodigious child, can only be as good as the information (data) it was trained on. This can change (and improve or get worse) over time but plenty of factors play into its training and the eventual bias or personality that emerges.
- Users should be mindful of how AI models like ChatGPT can inadvertently learn biases present in the data they were trained on, leading to biased language, stereotypes, or preferential treatment of certain topics. As responsible users, we should take active steps to contribute to the constant improvement of these models.
- Although OpenAI and other companies and research labs take steps to handle your data and chat history with care, you can't just leave such a responsibility to a third party. So safeguarding privacy and security is crucial when using AI, as sensitive information should not be provided to language models like ChatGPT, and we as users should adhere to best practices for data protection.
- Knowing this risk of bias is important in itself, so you can be mindful of taking steps to participate in its constant improvement, but also so that it will directly help you in your interactions with it.
- AI will have a far bigger impact on people's lives than social media and "fake news". It is important to use AI responsibly, employing ChatGPT ethically, fairly, and non- discriminatorily, considering the potential impact of generated content on individuals and communities.
- AI regulation, guidelines, and content detection mechanisms are important for ensuring ethical AI usage, as well as maintaining a

balance between innovation and ethical responsibility in a way that is safe, ideally growing aligned with human values and interests, and does not impede beneficial AI progress.

- Techniques for privacy have been developed that can help preserve privacy while allowing AI models like ChatGPT to learn from data; but ultimately it is up to users to actively maintain a positive attitude towards ethical usage and fight the complacency that is all too easy to allow.
- Remember that AI has a way of amplifying everything– good and bad– so extra care must be taken to accommodate them.

Action steps

After gaining insights and understanding from this chapter, you are equipped to use your ChatGPT skills responsibly and ethically. It's important to reflect on the principles you've learned and apply them to your interactions with ChatGPT.

- Reflect on the principles learned in this chapter and apply them to your interactions with ChatGPT.
- Take the concepts discussed in this chapter and resolve to apply the concepts discussed in this chapter in your usage of ChatGPT as well as any interactions with AI.
- Think about what changes you may likely make to your prompting process based on what has been discussed.
- Prepare for the next chapter to learn advanced techniques and strategies for ChatGPT mastery by reflecting on what you've already learned, and considering what concepts you'd need to adjust to apply them.

CHAPTER 6
STAYING AHEAD IN THE AI LANDSCAPE

"The best way to predict the future is to invent it."
— *Alan Kay*

"The illiterate of the 21st century will not be those who cannot read and write, but those who cannot learn, unlearn, and relearn."
— *Alvin Toffler*

Oh, AI, you big, beautiful, prodigious offspring of human ingenuity, poised to redefine the world. We're talking about a revolution to rival those of agriculture, industry, computing, and the internet. But let's be honest, this AI uprising might just steal the show, putting all other transformations to shame as it ushers in an era of unprecedented changes - the good, the bad, and the downright confusing.

Once upon a time, the realm of AI research resembled a chaotic buffet of ideas, where labs were like culinary islands, each cooking up their own unique albeit unshareable dishes. Computer vision aficionados whipped up delectable yet isolated feasts, while natural language processing (NLP) connoisseurs concocted a smorgasbord of obscure delights.

But then, like a culinary spawn of Simon Cowell and Gordon Ramsay yelling out nasties to boss everybody around while making others cry, large language models (LLMs) burst onto the scene, armed with their game-changing secret sauce. Google and OpenAI tinkered away behind closed doors for years until ChatGPT emerged, dazzling the world with its prowess that transcended dad jokes, and becoming the rallying point for a once fragmented field.

Suddenly, the AI community found itself with a grand unifying theory, and LLMs became like the coveted operating system upon which researchers and products could flourish. The key? Language. As ChatGPT demonstrated, language isn't just about words anymore; it's the backbone for understanding and translating all sorts of data.

From the visual language of images ,now transformed into tokens for computer vision models to the melodious language of music ripe for dissection by sophisticated audio algorithms, language has proven itself the veritable Swiss Army knife of AI, opening the world like its can opener, revealing the succulent contents within, carving intricate patterns of understanding, or tweezing apart the tangled threads of conversation to pluck out the pearls of wisdom hidden inside like an AI master chef cooking up the perfect virtual feast for our insatiable digital appetites.

And so now the AI revolution marches on, with a pace that has jet engines strapped to the marchers' boots, fueled by the power of language and the boundless potential of human curiosity, scaring the bejeezus out of even their own creators, but with potential benefits too great to consider putting a damper on its style.

Ahead of the Curve

Seriously, the field of AI language models is rapidly evolving, with new advancements continually pushing the boundaries of what is possible, at a dizzying, unprecedented pace.

For example, future advancements in AI language models may include improvements in unsupervised and self-supervised learning, multimodal learning, and the development of models that can reason and exhibit more human-like understanding. And that is but a tiny tip of the short-term iceberg— let alone the medium to longer-term ones— of rapid, strategic change that will be underway.

In this chapter, we will dive into ideas more than specific prompts about the rapidly advancing world of AI language models, to discover how to stay ahead of the curve, and become an unparalleled ChatGPT master in an ever-changing landscape.

We'll discuss strategies for keeping up with AI advancements, adapting to new AI models, and understanding the potential impact of future trends in AI language models on consumers within the context of ChatGPT mastery; but also where it fits in the broader scope of the impact AI will have across industry, commerce, government, healthcare, and everywhere else.

Keeping Up with the Rapidly Evolving AI Landscape

As AI technology continues to advance rapidly even at breakneck speed, it is essential to stay informed about new developments and learn how to adapt to new models and features. Staying informed and up-to-date is crucial for leveraging the full power of AI language models like ChatGPT because there will always be incremental and maybe sometimes in spurts, revolutionary advances that will help you produce better results with prompts and otherwise.

One way to stay informed is by following reputable AI research organizations and news outlets that focus on AI advancements. Examples include OpenAI, Google DeepMind, and MIT's Technology Review. Don't worry if you find the text dry or intimidating, there will usually be something you can gain from a careful examination; and if not, there will be resources that should follow to help you do the same, from articles and blogs to YouTube videos laying out the innovation and its greater impact.

Additionally, participating in online AI communities, forums, and social media groups where experts and enthusiasts alike share knowledge, discuss new developments, and exchange ideas is a great way to stay connected. Check out Facebook groups, Substack newsletters, Discord servers, or Twitter accounts that are known AI bellweathers, for example. This is rapidly evolving so any specific suggestion can get stale fast, so it is best to check them out yourself and search or find the recommendations from others.

Attending AI conferences, webinars, and workshops can also provide insights from industry leaders, offer networking opportunities with fellow AI enthusiasts, and broaden your understanding of the field.

Finally, it's essential to keep an eye on AI-related legislation and policy changes that may affect how you can use AI technology and the ethical implications of its use. Or how to adjust your prompt or settings at times when you need to squeeze information (legally of course) through circumventing the guardrails placed by AI companies.

Adapting to new AI models and features

As new AI models and features emerge in what will only be an accelerating pace, it's essential to adapt your prompting techniques and practices to make the most of these innovations. You don't need a degree in rocket science or keep your nose to the news grinder 24/7, but to stay nimble, experiment with new features and models as they become available, adjusting your prompting strategies to leverage their unique capabilities.

Seek out case studies, tutorials, and user guides that demonstrate the most effective ways to use new AI models and features. Then seek out analyses in articles, blog posts, newsletters and videos of the same general theme, including about those same specific case studies to give you deeper context and understanding about them.

Above all, maintain a growth mindset by being open to change and willing to learn from your experiences as you adapt to new AI technologies.

Here are some tips for adapting to new models and features:

- Understand, examine, and seek out the differences between AI model versions, and their implications.
- Experiment and drill yourself with new features and functionalities, including trying different wild variations of them to probe and test its limits and effects.
- Update your prompting strategies based on new capabilities not just as something you do sporadically but rather as a kind of philosophy, and regular regime.
- Learn from the experiences of other users by keeping abreast from articles, blog posts, social media sources like groups or individual Twitter accounts, for example.
- Share your own insights, because more often than not, doing so has the ancillary effect of allowing you to distill as well as organize your thinking resulting in a deeper understanding of what you're doing, while the feedback, conversations and advice from others will open up whole new doors to concepts and use-cases you may not have expected before. You can do these across one or different types of communities such as forums, social media, newsletters and posts, among many others.
- Nothing is ever etched in stone, so constantly be prepared to reevaluate your approach as AI continues to evolve.

One area to emphasize: Share it.

"**If you want to learn** something, read about it. **If you want to understand** something, write about it. **If you want to master something**, teach it." – Yogi Bhajan

You can argue that this is what I am doing, but you'd do yourself a big favor and accelerate your learning by living this philosophy.

How To Bypass AI Detectors and Create Undetectable AI

Let's get this out of the way first: AI should be used as a tool, not a replacement for a human writer, serving as a supplement to your creativity, not a replacement for it.

I say this not to be a lecturing schoolmarm yapping about ethics and sentimentality. No, I say this because although AI is already doing great and will continue to only improve at a pace faster than a politician can grab hold of a baby to kiss it, the thing is, AI detectors are also on a similar pace in their ability to detect AI generated content faster than you can say "polygraph."

What this means is that even if you used the latest gizmo or trick that uses some quantum-computing signal switcher from another universe, eventually the detectors will catch up, and if your content or material is dependent on seeming human, if they don't get you now, they'll still get you later. And if you've been in a field like the SEO business long enough, chasing after the latest tricks eventually becomes a fool's errand. Instead, establishing good practices early on will help make your content more enduring.

As such, there are two sets of strategies to take advantage of AI yet still make your content genuinely human. It will still take a good amount of work from you, but it will be a whole lot less then you used to do before, and produce superior results:

- *Method 1*) Utilize AI as a superpower-induced tool, and still ultimately write the content yourself; and
- *Method 2*) Optionally, let the AI also write your content whether it's an article, manuscript, report, slide, email, what have you and utilize

techniques anyway to mitigate or downright outmaneuver the AI detectors and whip them into submission.

Method 1: AI as Your Super Tool

The key to happiness as a user of ChatGPT, if you're a maker or creator of content, is using AI to enhance your writing process without replacing your own creativity. Be clever like a fox without losing your humanity. This approach requires embracing AI as your super tool, speeding up your workflow, and in the process, producing even better content, effectively harnessing ChatGPT's power so you can streamline your writing process and maintain your unique voice.

Think of yourself as an artist that still does the art yourself, but unlike the old days when you had to scour, grind and mix your own paints as well as stretch your own canvas, these days, digital tools help you erase, make and use different digital brushes on the fly, create new effects and many more. And even if you're doing it traditionally, that means you simply buy your materials from the store instead of making them, then be on your way planning and starting to draw or paint. That is, you don't have to be the one to hunt and kill your food yourself (it's an option!).

Here are some ways to use AI as your tool:

1. **Idea generation:** AI can help writers come up with new and interesting ideas for their writing projects by analyzing existing content and identifying patterns and themes.
2. **Research:** AI can assist in gathering and analyzing data from various sources, saving writers time and effort in conducting research.
3. **Outlining:** AI can help writers organize their thoughts and ideas into a cohesive outline, allowing them to see the big picture and structure of their writing project.

4. **Editing:** AI can be used to help writers identify and correct errors in their writing, such as grammar and spelling mistakes, inconsistencies, and awkward phrasing.
5. **Translation:** AI can assist in translating written content from one language to another, making it accessible to a wider audience.
6. **Content optimization:** AI can analyze the performance of written content and suggest optimizations to improve engagement, readability, and SEO.
7. **Voice dictation:** AI-powered voice recognition technology can be used to transcribe spoken words into written text, making it easier for writers to capture their ideas and thoughts on the go.
8. **Brainstorming:** AI-generated output can be used to generate ideas, prompts, and even plot lines for writers. This can help writers break through creative blocks and generate fresh perspectives on their work.
9. **Planning:** AI can assist writers in outlining their work, organizing their ideas, and developing a clear structure for their writing projects.
10. **Data gathering:** AI can help writers gather research and analyze data, which can be used to enhance the accuracy and credibility of their writing.
11. **Testing/Debating:** AI-generated output can be used to simulate debates or arguments on controversial topics, allowing writers to explore different points of view and test their arguments against various counterarguments.
12. **Translation:** AI can assist writers in translating their work into different languages, which can be beneficial for reaching wider audiences and expanding the impact of their writing.
13. **Editing and Proofreading:** AI-powered writing tools can help writers catch errors in their work, improve readability, and offer suggestions for improvements, ultimately leading to more polished and refined writing.

14. **Content Generation:** While not direct content creation, AI can generate content summaries, highlights, and topic models to assist writers in creating effective content that is targeted to their audience.

Method 2: Use AI to Create Content and Perform AI Detection Avoidance

In this method you (mostly) use the AI to create the content you intend anyway, then take steps before or after to maximize, optimize and cover all your bases.

While we must rise to the challenge and prove that true creativity is exclusively human, if you must, then use this method as your trusty sidekick, packed with techniques to outmaneuver AI detectors and sprinkle some human-sounding charm into your writing. With a dash of wit, a pinch of humor, and a hearty helping of ingenuity, we'll triumph over the machines and safeguard the authenticity of the written word... with the help of machines. (Oh well...)

Instead of listing the latest tricks that may work today but fail tomorrow, I'll provide you with more evergreen guidelines on best practices and principles that should endure even as detectors progress alongside large language models.

When using AI-generated content, pay attention to these evergreen guidelines:

1. Perplexity and Burstiness. The first telltale sign that differentiates human written text: Perplexity measures the relative chaos or randomness in the text, essentially how structurally complex a text is. On the other hand, burstiness compares the variation between sentences where AI text follows a more consistent pattern of style, length and so on, while human-written text generally does not take this into consideration where the idea being conveyed takes priority. To oversimplify it, perplexity is to words what burstiness is

to sentences. The lower the values for these two factors, the more likely it is that a text was produced by an AI, and vice versa, the higher they are, the better the likelihood of being human-made.

2. Rewrite your content using a tool like Use *Undetectable.ai* (https://undetectable.ai) or *QuillBot* (https://quillbot.com): Revise the text without changing its fundamental meaning while AI-generated text sound more natural and less robotic. Feel free to repeat the process multiple times to create a completely new version. Where there is decay and the words start sounding more and more strange as you refresh, change them yourself in the trouble spots without having to deal with the entire document in its entirety.

3. Break content into smaller segments: Generate each section separately, giving it a more natural feel, reviewing and editing each segment to improve text quality, add nuances, and incorporate variations typical of human conversation.

4. Avoid repetition and formulaic language: Vary sentence structure using different connecting words or phrases, including the use of synonyms, antonyms, or related words to avoid repeating the same words or phrases. Steer clear of cliches or common phrases; and express ideas in your own words.

5. Add a personal touch: Incorporate personal anecdotes or experiences to prove your knowledge of the subject. Make the text relatable and memorable for readers while supporting your main points or arguments with illustrative examples.

6. Check the content yourself with an AI detection tool like Originality.ai to identify any instances of AI-generated content or plagiarism. Correct flagged areas before using the text for its intended purpose, and to ensure your content is authentic, not just a copy of something else. Don't rely on this too much, that you get complacent and leave out subtle issues in your content until it gets into trouble at the next update.

7. Embrace your creativity: Infuse your work with originality and soul by letting your creative juices flow in the various ways you can add to the content in style, voice, content and soul; remembering that nothing beats the unique touch of a human writer, even if most of what you add or adjust are done in relative haste.

8. Leverage varying levels of formality: Like the point on patterns, and similar to burstiness and perplexity above, AI- generated content often sticks to a consistent level of formality, which can make it easy to detect. By consciously mixing formal and informal language or employing a conversational tone, you can make your writing appear more human, and have the good side-benefit of being more relatable and enjoyable.

9. Collaborate with others: Engage with fellow writers or colleagues to review, edit, and contribute to your content, even if only to see if they can detect any hints of AI in your content. This is a bit more trouble than you may want and not always available, but worth taking if you're able, because incorporating multiple human perspectives and writing styles elevates you to create a more diverse and authentic final product that is less likely to be flagged as AI-generated.

10. Regularly update your AI tools: Stay informed about the latest advancements and updates to your AI writing tool, the way SEO practitioners keep abreast of every scratch, snort, sneeze, or giggle that comes out of Google; and for the most part, it works. As AI technology evolves, the most up-to-date versions will be better equipped to generate human-like text, making it more difficult for detectors to identify your content as AI-generated, but never an excuse to be complacent because for both sides, the next update is always just around the corner.

Future Trends in AI Language Models and their Impact on Consumers

The future of AI language models promises exciting developments that will have a profound impact everywhere that could revolutionize how we interact with technology, not just in industry, labs or institutions but all the way to consumers themselves.

One potential trend is the development of multimodal AI models that can process and generate not only text but also images, audio, and video. For consumers, this could mean more interactive and immersive AI experiences and AI-generated content across different media types, but more importantly, a broader range of methods the AI can take input, process, and output a broader spectrum of insights.

Improved reasoning and understanding in AI models is another possible trend, increasing the incredible scope they can already deliver today, and especially when more solutions to token limitations arrive. As AI models become more capable of reasoning and demonstrating human-like understanding, consumers can expect more accurate, nuanced, and contextually relevant responses from AI language models like ChatGPT.

Enhanced customization and personalization capabilities are another area where AI language models will advance. ChatGPT is great at helping you ideate on your next presentation, provide ideas for your work, or summarize emails, for example. But AI models could become better at understanding individual users' preferences, leading to more personalized and tailored interactions in a way beyond using AI as a companion or romantic conversational partner or still doing that but at a far deeper level. Already people have fallen in love with their disembodied chatbots; imagine when these evolve to be even more personal, optimized for intimacy. It's scary but a huge boon for the beneficiaries.

This deeper integration into our lives also leads to another outcome: greater integration with other AI systems and services. While early examples have shown a kind of primitive (but still highly powerful) connectivity between disparate AI models, they will eventually have a seamless integration with each other, leading to massive effects, including end-to-end fulfillment of a prompter's desire and an outcome that today may seem too complicated or require complicated steps, but that these models will essentially cover by prompting itself or making prompts for instances of its own AI agents (already done today), to a seamless flow that seeks out complete solutions without you needing to specify them.

Moreover, as the importance of ethical AI becomes more widely recognized, we can expect improvements through shifts in regulatory frameworks and ethical considerations, including AI fairness, bias reduction, and data security. This leads to more responsible and trustworthy AI interactions for consumers, while the arms race continues as bad actors will surely also use AI to pursue their deeds, from new ways to scam people of their money or the likes of *deepfakes* either causing chaos for unfortunate targets or new ways to destroy democracy itself. We can only hope for the optimistic view of good actors being ahead of the curve.

Staying informed about the latest AI advancements, adapting to new models and features, and understanding future trends, ensure that you maintain your status and ability as a veritable ChatGPT master– not just for the status but for the innate ability to wrangle the most meat and performance from it– even as the AI landscape continues to evolve.

Self-Reflection and Continuous Improvement

As AI models advance, they are becoming capable of self-reflection and self-improvement, much like humans. Starting with GPT-4, this has significant implications for AI language models and their potential applications.

The self-reflection process and capability gaining attention starting with GPT-4 allows AI models to analyze its own performance, identify areas for improvement, and iteratively refine its responses. This enhances the model's accuracy, coherence, and relevance over time.

With self-reflecting AI, ChatGPT can improve its responses and adapt to individual users' preferences more effectively, providing a more personalized and satisfying user experience, especially when it can adjust its already impressive responses to be made even better.

Auto-GPT: Self-Prompting AI for Enhanced Functionality

Auto-GPT (and its brethren in AgentGPT, BabyAGI, GodMode, and Jarvis, among others) is among the first examples of an application that are essentially unsupervised learning AI tools or "AI agents" that can be given a goal by the user in natural language and will autonomously attempt to achieve it by breaking the goal into sub-tasks as well as creating its own prompts for sub-agents via the Internet and other tools in a continuous loop until it completes the task.

The self-prompting AI (or AI collective) takes language models a step further by allowing them to generate and execute new prompts based on initial input, leading to increasingly sophisticated responses and capabilities.

By combining self-prompting with other tools like web search and code execution, AI models can become more powerful assistants that provide end-to-end fulfillment of assignments, capable of performing complex tasks and providing more comprehensive assistance to users.

Auto-GPT and its ilk are incredibly impressive but are still in fact just the early examples of the potential to expand ChatGPT's capabilities far beyond text generation, making it an even more valuable resource for users in just about any field, able to handle a multitude of duties with a modicum of instructions (just make a clear prompt what you want and it will do the rest!).

ChatGPT is already like a tireless assistant (even the paid version is cheaper than cheap for the power it provides), yet the likes of Auto- GPT take this an order of magnitude higher with something seemingly scary good, but with benefits that are just too potentially great to ignore.

The Future of AI Collaboration

The future of AI language models will likely involve increased collaboration between AI systems, as well as between AI systems and humans.

Improved integration with other AI services will lead to more powerful, versatile, and interconnected AI ecosystems that can handle complex tasks with greater efficiency, and allow for more sophisticated instructions and .

On the other side of the AI collaboration coin is AI collaboration with humans where AI language models will likely become more focused on augmenting human capabilities, enabling humans and AI systems to work together seamlessly to achieve common goals or to simplify the interface between a human and AI that enables the easier, better ability to achieve more complicated, sophisticated demands and generate ever more effective results.

Explainable AI and Transparency

Today's AI is like a black box, in that they were built to learn with a combination of copious amounts of data, human assistance, and other innovations, enabling it to process all these in such an effective way that despite its imperfections still produce impressive results, yet ultimately its makers don't know the details and exact process by which it arrives at these results, making it challenging to comprehend how they arrive at their decisions or predictions.

The inputs and outputs are known, but the process of arriving at the output is unknown or unclear. And these have important implications when it comes to its applied contexts such as healthcare, finance, even self-driving cars, with the latter being a prime example of getting the blame for accidents in the field.

It is essential to explain how a decision was made, yet this is still proving to be an elusive goal.

As AI language models become more advanced and integrated into various aspects of our lives, the need for explainable AI and transparency in their decision-making processes remains extremely important, and increasingly so as the models become even more sophisticated, complicated, and effective.

Users and stakeholders need to understand how AI language models arrive at their outputs, fostering trust in their use and facilitating the identification of potential biases or errors, while stronger attention to future developments in techniques for explainable AI show a promising march towards this direction.

These could involve incorporating explainability techniques such as local interpretable model-agnostic explanations (LIME) and SHapley Additive exPlanations (SHAP) to provide clearer insights into their decision-making processes. Don't let the acronyms scare you, as these are essentially ways that help us understand how artificial intelligence systems are making decisions.

LIME helps us understand how a specific prediction or decision was made by highlighting the important features that were considered by the AI system, while SHAP helps us understand how much each feature contributes to a specific decision or prediction.

Techniques like these are like a window into the AI system's decision-making process, allowing us to better understand how it works and why it makes certain decisions, allowing us to gain more trust in AI systems and ensure that they are making decisions that are fair, accurate, and understandable instead of giving you a big surprise when your AI-infused toaster becomes self-aware and starts calling itself SkyNet.

AI for Multimodal Communication

The evolution of AI language models extends beyond text-based communication to incorporate other modalities, such as images, audio, and video, allowing them to generate, understand, and respond to a broader range of inputs and outputs.

This provides for serious implications to ChatGPT and its capabilities, enabling it to provide more comprehensive assistance in various contexts, such as video and audio content generation, sentiment analysis across different media, and interaction with users through multiple channels.

We've already seen the incredible advances made by ChatGPT as a text input/output model. Imagine the difference when it goes beyond that and into the realm of powerful human senses.

In fact, it isn't just an "addition" of capabilities or modalities such as being able to process images and video, but entire new capabilities and applications– including those not yet available or even thought of– that are to follow. And a fundamental advance that could usher in whole new benefits (and risks).

AI and Education

Education in this context is not just a sector that AI will touch (as much as it will on a foundational level). It's about how it will transform the way humans learn in a way that our educational institutions never imagined.

AI language models have the potential to revolutionize education by providing personalized learning experiences, assisting teachers, and enabling more efficient knowledge acquisition. But it also has the potential to change and improve the pace by which people *learn*.

Speeding it up, or simply improving it at its heart so that humans learn more better through the AI-enabled improvement to the underpinnings of understanding and knowledge itself.

The modern education system has formal schooling divided into grades, subjects and curricula, with its roots in the Industrial Revolution of the late 18th and early 19th centuries as a means of preparing individuals for the workforce became widespread and in general use until today. As far as we know, this has always been the most effective system of preparing people for the workforce, imparting knowledge and refining expertise.

All of these were human made and for the most part, gone unquestioned. AI could change that.

Future AI advancements may lead to language models that adapt to individual learners' needs and preferences, creating customized lesson plans and learning materials. At the same time, AI language models could be used to help teachers identify gaps in students' understanding, provide personalized feedback, and automate administrative tasks, allowing educators to focus on teaching. These alone are a huge leap forward.

Yet for all the good these will do, it can go even further, not just in optimizing educational processes but questioning and then improving upon the core underpinnings of the system's philosophy, resulting in a new, better, more effective, and even faster way we educate ourselves and convey the knowledge forward.

Key Takeaways

- AI language models are becoming the fundamental building block from which new innovations can be built upon, rapidly evolving and transforming various aspects of life.

- Being informed isn't enough: Staying informed and up-to- date is crucial for leveraging the full power of AI language models like ChatGPT.
- Be on a constant lookout: Adapt your prompting techniques and practices as new AI models and features emerge.
- Future trends in AI language models, such as multimodal learning, improved reasoning, and enhanced customization, will have profound impacts on consumers, and will even build upon itself and compound by improved models that do even more.
- It's an ongoing process: A growth mindset and continuous learning are essential to maintain mastery in the changing AI landscape.

Action Steps

- Follow reputable AI research organizations and news outlets.
- Participate in online AI communities, forums, and social media groups.
- Attend AI conferences, webinars, and workshops.
- Stay informed on AI-related legislation and policy changes.
- Experiment with new AI features and functionalities.
- Update your prompting strategies based on new capabilities. Drill, drill, drill.
- Learn from and share your experiences with others in the AI community.
- Reflect on your AI journey and embrace continuous improvement.
- Stay curious about the future of AI collaboration, explainable AI, multimodal communication, and AI's role in education.

CHAPTER 7
MASTERING CHATGPT AND EMBRACING THE FUTURE OF AI

"The greatest danger for most of us is not that our aim is too high and we miss it, but that it is too low and we reach it."
— *Michelangelo*

"The art and science of asking questions is the source of all knowledge."
— *Thomas Berger*

Mastering advanced ChatGPT prompting will revolutionize communication, work, and entertainment, and staying informed and adaptable in this rapidly changing landscape is the key to success.

This book has aimed to provide a comprehensive guide to mastering ChatGPT and prompt engineering for consumers. Throughout the chapters, we've covered the theories and principles behind good prompt engineering, provided a multitude of examples to hammer the concepts home, and presented the story behind the topics discussed, including the history and relevant background of the company and pertinent history as it pertains to ChatGPT.

We've also touched on issues like AI alignment and ethics that although not directly related to ChatGPT itself are nonetheless important in navigating the rapidly evolving landscape. This book has been structured so you gain the benefits regardless of your objectives— whether you want a broad grasp of the environment, or specific prompts and examples.

Most importantly, I cannot emphasize enough and encourage you to continue learning and exploring the ever-evolving world of AI, and take an active approach to doing this because AI isn't just a technology, it isn't just a tool, and it isn't just an impressive example of the celebration of amazing things the human mind can do. It's all of that and more, much more. With implications and great changes underway that are now clear, with yet more changes— good and bad that will fundamentally shape not just the future, but our changing place in it.

The transformative potential of advanced ChatGPT prompting

As AI language models continue to improve, advanced prompting techniques will unlock new opportunities and transform various aspects of our lives, including communication, work, and entertainment. Enhanced efficiency and effectiveness in communication will be one of the most notable transformations, as AI models like ChatGPT can assist in drafting emails, writing reports, and even translating languages. Additionally, AI-generated prompts can accelerate innovation and creative problem-solving, pushing the boundaries of human imagination.

Improved access to information and knowledge is another crucial aspect of advanced ChatGPT prompting. AI language models can help condense large amounts of data, making it easier for users to access and understand complex information. Furthermore, the empowerment of individuals and businesses through AI technology will lead to increased productivity, more informed decision-making, and better overall outcomes.

Conclusion

In the rapidly evolving world of AI, the accelerating pace of its trajectory, and the already explosive nature of development in its space, it's almost a platitude but a simple truth: staying informed and adaptable is crucial for success.

Staying informed about AI advancements and future trends will ensure that you remain at the forefront of the AI landscape, ready to adapt and leverage new technologies as they emerge, as we have covered in Chapter 6. Reading this book means you are already embracing the transformative potential of AI, so with the greater powers available to you in part from what you've gained from reading, I would encourage you to use it responsibly, considering the ethical implications of AI use and ensuring that you be a part– no matter how small or how big– and contribute to a future where AI technology benefits all.

With the conclusion of this book, you are now equipped (and hopefully, inspired) to master ChatGPT and prompt engineering. Remember that the journey of learning and discovery in the AI landscape is ongoing, and mastery is a continuous process. Ultimately, your dedication to continued learning and growth will be the key to unlocking the full potential of ChatGPT and other AI technologies.

Key Takeaways

- Advanced prompting techniques like those you've learned in this book go beyond the usual ways people use ChatGPT and have the potential to go beyond mere answers (already amazing in themselves) to truly transform various aspects of our lives, including communication, work, and entertainment.
- Staying informed about AI advancements and future trends will help you remain at the forefront of the AI landscape, able to adapt to changing circumstances, and ahead of the curve long before others take notice.

- Improved access to information and knowledge is a crucial aspect of advanced ChatGPT prompting. This book lays the foundation, and your ongoing process matters just as much. (See below.)
- Mastery is a continuous process, and dedication to continued learning and growth is essential.

Action Steps

- Reflect on your journey thus far and identify areas where you are able to compose more effective prompts, and where you can improve your ChatGPT prompting skills.
- Stay up-to-date with the latest advancements in AI technology and make a habit of incorporating new techniques into your prompting repertoire.
- Continuously seek opportunities to learn and grow, embracing the challenge of mastering ChatGPT and other AI technologies.
- Join AI-related communities, like forums or groups, to engage in discussions, ask questions, and share your experiences with like-minded individuals.
- As you embark on your journey to mastery, always keep in mind the ethical implications of AI use, and strive to contribute to a future where AI technology benefits all. Doing this may allow you to reap benefits to your specific use.

LEAVE A REVIEW

Thank you so much for purchasing my book and for making it all the way to the end!

Before you go, I wanted to ask you for one small favor. Could you please consider posting a review on the platform? Posting a review is the best and easiest way to support the work of independent authors like me.

If you enjoyed d this book, I'd really appreciate it if you left your honest feedback. I love hearing from my readers, and I personally read every single review.

Your feedback will help me to keep writing the kind of books that will help you get the results you want. It would mean a lot to me to hear from you.

BONUS CHAPTERS

NOTEWORTHY CONCEPTS TO MAKE PROMPTING CHATGPT EVEN BETTER

APPROACHES

"The path to knowledge branches in many directions."
— *Francis Bacon*

There are many ways to skin the cat that is ChatGPT. It works wonders when appropriately prompted, but getting the most out of conversations requires skill. There are countless reports of chatbots like it that drift off course when asked for too much. This chapter delves into more of the noteworthy approaches used by the pros that you can use to steer ChatGPT interactions and strum it like a virtuoso.

First, "tree-of-thought" prompting structures dialogue like branch points on a map. This allows users to cover more ground without losing the plot, guiding the conversation through a fluid branching structure personalized to the user's goals and the chatbot's capabilities.

Next, "multimodal" prompting incorporates images, audio, and video to ground AI in real-world contexts. Diverse sensory data stimulates richer discourse.

Finally, "meta-prompting" strategically sequences a series of shorter prompts to complement the AI's strengths and limitations to tackle challenges beyond its normal scope. It effectively sequences shorter prompts as stepping stones, leading ChatGPT through stepped interactions suited to its attributes. This unlocks more ambitious results by strategically building on its strengths.

It's important to remember that while these strategies can enhance the interaction with ChatGPT, we are working within the limits of the AI's training data, algorithms, and inherent capabilities. These can sometimes lead to unpredictable, albeit generally effective, results. The strategies laid out in this chapter help unlock more ambitious results by strategically building on its strengths.

Knowing how to speak its inner language is like mastering the secret chords that bring out its strongest magic, and with these approaches, you'll guide discussions much further than most users and derive the most effective results.

Tree-of-Thought

Tree-of-thought prompting is a more involved but effective method for interfacing with large language models (LLMs) like ChatGPT. The basic premise is to break down problems into a tree-like structure, with each node representing a step in the problem-solving process. This allows the AI to explore possible solutions to a problem and backtrack if a particular solution is not working.

So, instead of feeding ChatGPT a single prompt, the user structures a tree of interrelated prompts mapped to the AI's capabilities to explore it dynamically and leverage its strengths based on comprehension, interests, and reasoning.

This tree-structured set of prompts forms an evolving conceptual map that ChatGPT can traverse during the conversation. The initial root prompt is the broadest starting point, typically an open-ended topic or question. This then branches out into sub-topics, details, and follow-up questions that split further into more granular child branches. Each branch and sub-branch represents a conceptual waypoint for the AI to pursue within the confines of the wider prompt-tree architecture defined by the user.

An Example Prompt Tree

Let's put it in simple, broader terms first, and afterward, I'll make another example in a more structured form to drive the message home. As a basic example, the root of the prompt tree could be "Explain quantum computing at a high level." The first branch could be "Provide background on the origins and development of quantum computing." Another branch could be "Explain some of the key principles that make quantum computers different." Each level of one branch could be split further, with quantum principles breaking down into specifics like superposition, entanglement, and quantum parallelism.

By providing this tree-based prompting structure rather than linear scripts, the user and the AI agent take a path through the information based on its dynamic assessment of priority topics. If the AI does not fully grasp the superposition concept, it may explore and elaborate on the branches related to that sub-topic before moving to other areas of the prompt tree. Or if, through earlier dialogue, the AI determines that quantum computing applications align strongly with the user's interests, it may devote more attention to traversing that branch.

Like a loose, AI prompting version of a mind map, the user interacts with the AI to cultivate a custom "knowledge tree," pruning off irrelevant tangents and prompting for deeper insight where useful. ChatGPT, in turn, directs its curiosity as it engages with this steadily adapting structure, resulting in a more alive, coherent, and mutually fulfilling dialogue than scripted question-response sequences.

This approach provides multiple benefits:

1. More control and adaptability based on user interests since any branch can be expanded or narrowed fluidly to solve a problem.

2. Reduced repetition, as the AI has the freedom to take the conversation in less predictable directions.
3. Easy zooming in/out on topics by nesting prompts at various conceptual levels.
4. More logical, on-topic responses as the AI's reasoning is bounded by the prompt framework.
5. Reusable prompt tree structures for iterating on concepts across sessions.

Another Example:

Now that you've gotten familiar with the method, here's another example.

Root:

Prompt:

"Please explain machine learning concepts to me at a basic level."

Branch 1:

Prompt:

"Provide some background and real-world context first."

Possible ChatGPT Responses:

- Everyday examples relying on machine learning
- Future possibilities and impact

Branch 2:

Prompt:

"Now give an overview of how machine learning works."

Possible ChatGPT Responses:

- Different types of ML approaches
- Data, algorithms, training

- Strengths vs weaknesses

Branch 3:

Prompt:

"Can you clarify some key terminology?"

Possible ChatGPT Responses:
- Supervised, unsupervised reinforcement
- Features, classification, predictions
- Overfitting, underfitting
- Clear examples for each term

From here, you can proceed with more granularity until you reach a satisfactory outcome or keep going further.

It is essential to know that crafting effective prompt trees is as much art as science. It relies on finding the right balance between clearly delineating conceptual waypoints at branch points while keeping the framework flexible enough for the AI to inject its connections and insights. Trees that are too rigid or complex quickly lose coherence. The user must also be careful not to constrain the AI too firmly or risk dulling its curiosity.

With careful prompt engineering, though, this approach can feel like an unscripted journey through a conceptual garden guided jointly by humans and AI. Both participate in selectively cultivating its growth towards shared understanding and while missteps are inevitable, simply backtracking and pruning troublesome branches often puts the dialogue back on track.

In Summary

Tree-of-thought prompting aims to channel key strengths of the AI through a fluid branching prompt structure tailored by the user.

Carefully branching interest-aligned questions can inspire more dynamic and mutually enriching dialogue.

However, it is essential to remember that humans guide dialogues through prompt crafting while ChatGPT responds based on training limitations. Tree-of-thought prompting steers conversations by aligning prompts to AI capabilities – not by fundamentally improving the model. ChatGPT doesn't internally maintain a tree structure of the dialogue; instead, it generates responses based on the immediate context (the last few messages) and its training without an internal conceptual map. While this approach can guide ChatGPT to cover different areas of a topic, the effectiveness is still dependent on the AI's training and knowledge limitations. In other words, it's a valuable method for guiding the conversation but doesn't fundamentally change how the AI processes information.

Key takeaways:

- Tree-of-thought prompting structures AI-human dialogue through branching prompt sets.
- Allows dynamically cultivating curiosity-driven conversations.
- Balances guidance at branch points with the agency for the AI.
- It feels more natural and fulfilling than rigid scripts.
- Proper prompt engineering is challenging but critical.
- Tree-of-thought prompting is more of a conceptual framework, not an internal structure.

Action steps:

- Identify an open-ended topic for the initial prompt tree.
- Craft 1-2 level branches on logical sub-topics.
- Develop 3-5 sub-branches for key concepts under those.
- Converse with ChatGPT while adaptively editing the tree.
- Save effective trees for future re-use.

Exercises:

1. Construct a 5-level prompt tree to explain a hobby or interest of yours to a beginner.
2. Practice conversing with ChatGPT while adaptively editing branches based on its responses.
3. Analyze an existing dialogue and identify how it could have been improved with tree branching.

Assignments:

- Develop a conceptual prompt tree to walk a child through solving a multi-step math word problem.
- Build an immediate hierarchy to help ChatGPT compose a short poem about a memorable life event.

Answers to Exercises

Exercise 1. Construct a 5-level Prompt Tree to Explain a Hobby or Interest of Yours to a Beginner

Example Hobby: Astronomy

Level 1: Introduction to Astronomy

- Prompt: What is astronomy, and why is it important?

Level 2: Basic Concepts in Astronomy

- What are the different celestial bodies we can see in the night sky?
- How do telescopes help in astronomy?

Level 3: Exploring the Solar System

- Can you tell me about the planets in our solar system?
- What are comets and asteroids?

Level 4: Deep Sky Objects and Advanced Topics

- What are galaxies, and how are they different from stars?
- Can you explain black holes and supernovas?

Level 5: Practical Aspects of Astronomy

- How can a beginner start observing the night sky?
- What are some resources to learn more about astronomy?

Exercise 2. Practice Conversing with ChatGPT While Adaptively Editing Branches Based on Its Responses

- **Initial Prompt:** Tell me about the basics of gardening.
- **ChatGPT Response:** [Explains soil, sunlight, and water requirements]
- **Adapted Prompt:** What are common beginner mistakes in gardening?
- **Further Adaptation:** How can I create a simple herb garden at home?

Exercise 3. Analyze an Existing Dialogue and Identify How It Could Have Been Improved with Tree Branching

Example Dialogue:

- You: How do I make a cake?
- ChatGPT: [Explains basic cake recipe]
- You: What if it doesn't rise properly?

Improved with Tree Branching:

- **Initial Prompt:** Tell me about baking a cake.
- **Branch 1:** What are the essential ingredients in a cake?
- **Branch 2:** What are common issues while baking a cake and how do you solve them?
- **Sub-branch:** What to do if a cake doesn't rise properly?

Multimodal Prompting

Enhancing ChatGPT Through Multi-Sensory Context

In 2023, OpenAI introduced various features in the paid ChatGPT Plus subscription, including features permitting the AI to interpret visual, auditory, and interactive signals alongside text prompts. This multisensory context grounds AI reasoning in real-world knowledge, yielding more insightful dialogue and enabling prompts to become information-rich reflections of multifaceted real-world data by incorporating images, diagrams, audio, video, and interactive elements.

Rather than purely textual descriptions, multimodal prompts allow ChatGPT to observe scenarios more akin to human experience. For example, assisting with a question on football is far smoother by showing gameplay footage than engaging through words alone.

Multimodality helps address inherent limitations with text-only training by exposing ChatGPT to the complexity of the physical world. Reasoning rooted in actual visuals, sounds, and interactions is more contextually aligned than just stringing plausible words together.

Crafting these multimodal prompts introduces new challenges compared to text alone, especially regarding data volume and diversity. But continued progress in computer vision, speech recognition, and generative media rapidly expands the possibilities. Just as important is knowing that this is not a mere incremental feature dropped in place but an integrated component with a deeper contextual value, proven by how modern language models like ChatGPT have shown the ability to integrate and reason more qualitatively over various input modes in an integrated way once trained on the right data.

Multimodal prompting enhances language models like ChatGPT through:

- Richer context from diverse real-world sensory signals.
- Grounding word-based reasoning in physical world knowledge.

- Capturing data too complex for textual description alone.
- Language model architectures adapted for cross-modal fusion.

The result is that ChatGPT is better equipped to understand human requests, explain concepts clearly with supporting evidence, describe real or imagined scenes with sharper precision and insight, and unlock ChatGPT's next level of conversational insight.

Examples

Here are eight examples of multi-modal prompting. As of this writing, some functions are still in beta or require more elaborate workarounds (such as using ChatGPT's Code Interpreter or browser extensions to enable video as input), so results may vary, may result in an error or require additional tweaking and runs. But they illustrate the breadth of possibilities across different domains:

- **Summarize A Movie Plot** - Asking ChatGPT to summarize a movie by showing select images from a movie or the script.

  - Text: **The following video screencaps and script excerpts are from the movie [Title]. Please carefully examine them and provide a concise 3-4 sentence summary of the film's central plot points and themes.**
  - *[Attach/Insert screen captures or copy-paste longer descriptions taken online, for example.]*

- **Generate Recipes** - Using a slightly different, straightforward version from Grandma's example above; here you get recipes from ChatGPT by showing it images of the finished dish along with key ingredients.

  - Text: **Here is an image of [dish name]. Given this desired finished meal presentation and the list of key ingredients below, please formulate a detailed multi-step recipe with approximate cooking times and required tools to reproduce this dish.**

- *[Attach/Insert image of plated dish]*
- Text: (Optional) **Ingredients:** [list of ingredients]

- **Describe Historical Event** - Describe a historical event to ChatGPT using archived photos, audio interviews, and newspaper headlines related to the incident.

  - Text: **Please study the attached files to describe and summarize the key details around the [event name or historical incident] in 2-3 paragraphs.**
  - *[Attach/Insert relevant selection of photos, audio clips, and headlines formatted appropriately]*

- **Explain Physics Concept** - Explain physics concepts like velocity and friction by showing image demonstrations of objects moving.

  - Text: **The image attached demonstrates the physics concept of [key term]. Please analyze the depicted interactions and describe how they exemplify the relevant properties and formulas, including defining any additional physics terminology required to characterize what is demonstrated accurately.**
  - *[Attach/Insert an image of a physics concept being illustrated visually]*

- **Identify Objects in Images** - Identify objects in photos by providing ChatGPT example images labeled with the correct terms.

  - *[Attach/Insert one or more images of objects, people, animals, etc., with machine-readable labels atop each image]*
  - Text: **Please examine the images attached and describe in your own words the rationality of the interaction and how seemingly diverse objects have a logical connection.**

- **Answering Geography / Culture Questions** - Answering questions about geography and culture by displaying maps, diagrams, and images related to the location.

- Text: **Please examine the maps, diagrams, photos, numerical data, and textual information below related to [specific location] and then respond to the following questions:**
- *[Attach/Insert appropriately formatted selection of images, maps, and data tables regarding the specified geography/culture]*
- Example Questions:

1. Provide an overview of the distinctive geographic features of this location and how they influence local culture and economy.
2. Characterize and summarize key aspects of customs, heritage, architecture, community life, and other cultural traits based on the data provided.
3. Contrast and compare life in this area to comparable locations in neighboring regions.

- **Discuss a Health or Medical Case** - Discussing medical cases with ChatGPT can be tricky because of privacy and similar concerns, but careful considerations such as using a photo from your phone or uploaded file as examples depicting a condition such as a rash, bottle nutrition guides, or doctor analysis reports as an example, can provide valuable insights.

  - Text: **Examine the information presented and provide an overview of the likely diagnosis, open questions, recommended tests, and initial treatment considerations.**
  - *[Attach/Insert visual scan data or other relevant modalities]*

- **Data for Source References** - Adding high-resolution images, sketches, or references allows for conveying the concept. For example, an artist can use this to convey the dynamic play of light far better than text alone could describe. This grounds the basis in real-world textures, lighting angles, and motion ChatGPT can intelligently factor in.

  - Text: **Please provide tips for an amateur painter looking to capture more photorealistic detail based on these different**

images and sounds showcasing examples of sunlight streaming through trees.

- *[Attach/Insert various reference images of sunbeam lighting effects in the forest, paired with audio of animal life from the area]*

The possibilities span many domains as long as relevant multi-modal inputs are provided for grounding. The core goal remains enriching ChatGPT's context through diverse, quality-curated sensory inputs structured into prompts that fuse modalities into reasoning.

In Summary

The central concept of multimodal prompting is enhancing text prompts by adding related pictures, data files, or sounds. This gives the language model more complete and detailed real-life information to work with. Getting data through different senses like sight and hearing instead of just text helps the system better understand things like humans do. Providing these extra examples from the physical world helps the language model answer better.

Key Takeaways

- Text prompts alone limit real-world grounding.
- Multi-modal inputs provide a richer context.
- Diverse inputs improve language model performance.
- Fusing modalities enables more complex reasoning.
- Crafting quality training data remains challenging.
- Multimodal inputs may not be as nuanced as human perception (yet)

Action Steps

- Determine modalities needed beyond text (visual/audio/etc.).
- Source/generate diverse multi-modal datasets.
- Preprocess data (tagging, transcripts, etc.).

- Structure prompts to combine modalities.
- Prompt iteratively while monitoring output.
- Refine approaches to improve multi-modal reasoning.

Exercises:

- Enhance movie or recipe questions for ChatGPT with relevant images.
- Experiment with transcribing audio clips to inject as supplemental prompts.
- Evaluate improvements using images vs text-only for ambiguous prompts.

Assignments

- Curate a set of labeled photos to aid ChatGPT in describing your hometown to someone who has never visited.
- Record a short video to demonstrate a scientific concept when querying ChatGPT visually.

Meta-Prompting

Meta-prompting refers to strategically structuring a multi-step prompt sequence to complement areas where ChatGPT struggles with longer freeform conversations Rather than a single long request, it scaffolds guidance tuned to ChatGPT's strengths and limitations.

While this may sound sophisticated, it does not require complex AI - regular users can meta-prompt by drawing on their direct ChatGPT knowledge. Reflect on output types that shine versus where coherence falters after a few paragraphs. Armed with that insight, you may then scaffold prompts manually.

For example, ask ChatGPT to write a fantasy adventure. It may provide promising paragraphs before losing narrative focus. It might start strong with some good paragraphs, but the story often drifts or repeats later.

We can guide ChatGPT by breaking things into steps:

First, have it outline the key story beats chapter by chapter. ChatGPT handles logical plots well.

Next, pick one part outlined and ask for more creative details on the action. Like some vivid paragraphs around the main battle scene. Focused requests work better than saying, "Be creative!" all at once.

Finally, have it summarize everything to tie up loose ends and finish the tale. Short reflections are also easier for ChatGPT than longer threads.

Specifically, to help avoid going wayward, prompt with incremental guidance:

Prompt 1: "Outline a 5-chapter fantasy plot, including story arcs"

Prompt 2: "Expand the Chapter 3 conflict scene with vivid detail"

Prompt 3: "Summarize the full transformation arc in one paragraph"

Structuring prompts this way plays more to ChatGPT's strengths (facts, short bursts) while avoiding weaknesses (dragging on creatively).

Meta-Prompting Examples

Example 1. Writing a Children's Story

ChatGPT is sharp; able to summarize facts smartly and perform most of what you intend. Still, it may not seem very creative for extended narratives, and things like making creative stories without some help, for example, isn't its thing yet. After a few lines, its tales can get boring, while descriptive scenes and passages tend to turn repetitive fast.

Like if you said: "Write a children's story about a mouse meeting a rabbit, with imaginative details." Don't expect great stuff from its output.

But here's a trick that helps: Guide ChatGPT step-by-step:

1. First, ask for the basics.

    Prompt: "Describe the main things that happen in the mouse + rabbit story."

Keep it factual. ChatGPT will outline no problem.

2. Next, take one part outlined and prompt for creativity.

    Prompt: "For when they first meet, describe two things the mouse sees and two sounds it hears."

This pushes ChatGPT further but stays focused on one scene with specific asks, not just "Be creative!" all at once.

It leverages what ChatGPT can do easily (logical outlines) to help it later where it struggles (original immersive scenes). No frustration for either side!

Notice the critical aspects of this example:

- It has a helper system (the narrator) structuring prompts for ChatGPT
- The prompts are designed to complement ChatGPT's weaknesses (creativity)
- There is a scaffolding approach of more straightforward to more complex prompts
- The overall strategy attempts to optimize prompting itself

Rather than just providing a single prompt for the full children's story, the helper scaffolds the process:

1. Outlining the logical plot first (plays to ChatGPT's strengths)
2. Then, prompting for targeted creative descriptions (addresses weaknesses)

This directionality and structured enhancement of ChatGPT's capabilities reflects algorithmically generated prompts tuned to the model. At the same time, the layered prompting, scaffolding, and optimization of ChatGPT's skills exemplify a good meta-prompting approach.

The key is structuring prompts so you get the foundations laid before expecting fancier content on top. Trying to force it the other way around just risks collapsing. Guide the horse before charging forward!

Ultimately, it's about learning ChatGPT's strengths and weaknesses and prompts that complement both together, bit by bit. You can cross wider creative waters with simple stepping stones than forcing a flooded river upfront.

Example 2: Grandma's Cooking Buddy

Let ChatGPT act as a cooking assistant that helps Grandma digitize her loose-leaf paper recipes. But many ingredients are non-standard or ambiguous, like "some olive oil" or "dash of salt," or when she just wrote "butter" without saying how much butter exactly. Now ChatGPT is mad smart, but it may struggle to parse Grandma's handwritten recipes. So, let's help it along.

In this context, you can either type what Grandma wrote or, better yet, scan or take a photo of her notes and let ChatGPT recognize and process it with your added instructions as "Cooking Buddy." The goal is to digitize Grandma's handwritten recipe using ChatGPT without losing any nuance from Grandma's personalized ingredient descriptions.

A meta prompting assistant can structure the task like the below example prompts.

Prompts in sequence:

1. You are a cooking assistant called "Cooking Buddy." Please carefully review Grandma's handwritten oatmeal cookie recipe

text and this visual photo of the fully prepared cookies, taking notes on key traits about amounts and ingredients.

2. [Attach/include images of recipe text and photo of prepared cookies]

3. Now, transcribe the full textual recipe verbatim, leaving any vague amounts like 'butter' unchanged from Grandma's original description.

4. Enumerate any ingredients listed without precise objective amounts, quantities, volumes, or weights with the transcribed recipe.

5. For the 'butter' called for in the recipe, estimate a reasonable quantity by examining the recipe text details alongside the image example of butter sticks shown.

6. Translate any approximate volume amounts, like 'handful of raisins,' to measuring cup equivalents based on written description hints and visual appearance clues.

7. Please read back the full recipe with all ingredients converted to standardized measurement units while preserving Grandma's distinctive flavor notes.

The above prompt scaffolding helps the AI handle open-ended clarification dialogue while preventing it from glossing over ambiguous recipe details. Grandma is delighted by the fully digitized recipes!

Here's why the key meta-prompting aspects it demonstrates work:

1. There is an assistant AI ("Cooking Buddy") structuring prompts for the main AI (ChatGPT). This prompt engineering framework reflects the core idea behind meta-prompting.

2. The multi-step prompting scaffold purposefully complements ChatGPT's weaknesses with parsing ambiguous recipe ingredients/amounts. It is designed to optimize ChatGPT's capabilities.

3. Cooking Buddy is effectively learning an optimal prompting mechanism to digitize recipes using its understanding of ChatGPT's strengths and limitations.
4. The layering of more straightforward clarification prompts to more complex summarization prompts again reflects an algorithmic approach to decomposing a difficult conversational task.

How Cooking Buddy strategically responds to the prompts you tailored to guide ChatGPT through simplifying assumptions to open-ended requests constitutes meta-prompting's goal of learning specialized prompt generation algorithms. The iterative scaffolding and guidance tuned to the model epitomizes the automated optimization loop meta-prompting aims to achieve.

In Summary

The meta prompting strategy of breaking down complex tasks into more minor, more manageable prompts is a useful technique, especially for longer or more complex tasks.

The goal is to break things down into intuitive stepping stones tailored to how ChatGPT processes information best, emphasize intuitive process-based principles about scoping prompts, and leverage innate capabilities versus trying to overhaul them.

Rather than attempting advanced challenges all at once, you guide it in manageable chunks suited to its capabilities, course-correct when needed, and repurpose effective structures, effectively sequencing prompts to play to its strengths while circumventing shortcomings.

The success of meta-prompting heavily relies on the user's ability to understand and predict ChatGPT's strengths and limitations, ideally needing you to interpret its responses to structure effective follow-up prompts, just as you're learning in this chapter and the rest of the book.

Key Takeaways

- ChatGPT isn't perfect. It's a tool with strengths and weaknesses
- Breaking big requests down into steps works better
- Start with simple factual questions to get solid footing
- Slowly build up to more complex creative asks
- Check its output all along the way to keep things clear
- Re-word prompts to focus on things GPT handles well
- Adjust direction when responses get confusing
- Save good multi-step prompts to reuse later
- Avoid prompts that could lead to harmful, biased, or unethical outputs

Action Steps

- Note where ChatGPT loses steam or gets confused when asking for lots of creative content
- Break the big request into smaller bite-sized prompts
- Start with easy factual questions to get solid footing
- Then, build up to more complex tasks one step at a time
- Check ChatGPT's output along the way to ensure things make sense
- Adjust wording to focus on its strengths for each prompt
- Change framing if needed to help the flow
- Save effective multi-step prompt sequences to reuse

Exercises

1. Manually scaffold a fantasy fiction prompt in progressive steps per ChatGPT's capabilities
2. Break down an open-ended question into clarifying sub-questions before summarizing
3. Identify a scenario where tiered prompting could expand on deficiencies

Assignments

- Develop a multi-level prompt structure for composing lyrics to an original song
- Guide ChatGPT through multi-step reasoning to solve a budgeting challenge

Sample Answers to Exercises and Assignments

Exercises

1. *"Manually scaffold a fantasy fiction prompt in progressive steps per ChatGPT's capabilities"*

- Prompt 1: Outline five chapters, including the protagonist, worldbuilding, the central conflict
- Prompt 2: Describe three key senses the hero experiences entering the fantasy city
- Prompt 3: Script a 2 paragraph dialogue scene about the brewing political tensions
- Prompt 4: Detail the epic final battle scene with the evil wizard in five vivid sentences
- Prompt 5: Conclude with a paragraph tying up the hero's journey transformation

2. *"Break down an open-ended question into clarifying sub-questions before summarizing"* - Break down summarizing the history of AI into sub-questions

- When did the early conception of intelligent machines begin?
- What were pioneering developments leading to modern AI?
- How did machine learning and neural networks emerge?
- What fueled recent advances like large models?
- Now, summarize key milestones in one paragraph.

4. 3. *"Identify a scenario where tiered prompting could expand on deficiencies"* - Writing wedding invitation verses

- Prompt 1: Specify wedding style, theme, and values
- Prompt 2: Recommend phrasing for opening line setting stage
- Prompt 3: Craft a romantic metaphor incorporating style
- Prompt 4: Close expressing shared future hopes

Assignments

1. *"Develop a multi-level prompt structure for composing lyrics to an original song"* - Composing original song lyrics

- Prompt 1: Please suggest ideas for a song topic focus
- Prompt 2: Given [selected topic], offer five lyrical phrases expressing [related theme]
- Prompt 3: Provide a structural outline including verse 1 topic sentence, verse 2 elaboration, bridge contrast, chorus emotional peak
- Prompt 4: Populate verse 1 lyrics aligned to the provided structural outline
- Prompt 5: Populate verse 2 lyrics aligned to the provided structural outline

2. *"Guide ChatGPT through multi-step reasoning to solve a budgeting challenge"* - Guide reasoning through monthly budget

- Prompt 1: Categorize monthly fixed costs by rent, utilities, transport, etc.
- Prompt 2: Classify typical monthly variable spending on food, leisure, etc.
- Prompt 3: Given an average monthly income of $X, assess the feasibility of expenses
- Prompt 4: Propose discretionary cuts or changes if spending exceeds reasonable thresholds

- Prompt 5: Provide three final specific, actionable recommendations for creating a budget surplus going forward.

BONUS CHAPTER 2
PROMPT ENGINEERING GUIDE FROM OPENAI

> "If I had an hour to solve a problem, I'd spend 55 minutes thinking about the problem and 5 minutes thinking about solutions."
>
> — *Albert Einstein*

On December 17th, 2023, OpenAI produced its own prompt engineering guide. Consider it a good and definitive guide to prompting its models, including ChatGPT. However, it isn't intended to be exhaustive and encompassing and is meant to be a guide for developers using its API instead of the consumer ChatGPT web or mobile app.

This chapter seeks to fill that gap. Let's rework and dig into it using the official guide as canon to use the ChatGPT app (web or mobile) directly. Think of it as the guide for the ChatGPT user instead of an API user, with strategies and tactical prompt design principles to transform simple queries into masterful prompts that elicit ChatGPT's most accurate and in-depth responses.

(The official guide service as our basis is here: https://platform.openai.com/docs/guides/prompt-engineering/)

This guide notes that it "shares strategies and tactics for getting better results from large language models (LLMs, also as GPT models, per OpenAI) like GPT-4. The methods described here can sometimes be combined for greater effect, and we encourage experimentation to find the best methods for you." The guide also notes that some examples demonstrated "currently work only with our most capable model, GPT-4. In general, if you find that a model fails at a task and a more capable model is available, it's often worth trying again with the more capable model."

So, with that in mind, let's go over the guide as it applies to the ChatGPT (website/app) user.

Strategies for getting better results

Strategy 1. Write clear instructions

These models can't read your mind. If outputs are too long, ask for brief replies. If outputs are too simple, ask for expert-level writing. If you dislike the format, demonstrate the format you'd like to see. The less the model has to guess what you want, the more likely you'll get it.

You'd believe that is too basic even to include here, but you'd be surprised at the number of people that ignore this and how much better many results can be by following this really simple point.

Tactic: Include details in your query to get more relevant answers

To get a highly relevant response, ensure requests provide all essential details or context. Otherwise, you leave it up to the model to guess what you mean.

Worse	Better
How do I add numbers in Excel?	How do I add up a row of dollar amounts in Excel? I want to do this automatically for a whole sheet of rows with all the totals ending up on the right in a column called "Total."

Who's president?	Who was the president of Mexico in 2021, and how frequently are elections held?
Write code to calculate the Fibonacci sequence.	Write a TypeScript function to calculate the Fibonacci sequence efficiently. Comment the code liberally to explain what each piece does and why it's written that way.
Summarize the meeting notes.	Summarize the meeting notes in a single paragraph. Then, write a Markdown list of the speakers and their key points. Finally, list the next steps or action items suggested by the speakers, if any.

Tactic: Use delimiters to indicate distinct parts of the input

Delimiters, like triple quotation marks, XML tags, section titles, etc., can help restrict sections of text to be treated differently.

Example 1:

Prompt:

> *Summarize the text delimited by triple quotes with a haiku.*
>
> *"""insert text here"""*

Example 2:

Prompt:

> *You will be provided with a pair of articles (delimited with XML tags) about the same topic. First, summarize the arguments of each article. Then, indicate which of them makes a better argument and explain why.*
>
> *<article> insert first article here </article>*
>
> *<article> insert second article here </article>*

Example 3:

Prompt:

> *You will be provided with a thesis abstract and a suggested title. The thesis title should give the reader a good idea of the topic of the thesis but should also be eye-catching. If the title does not meet these criteria, suggest five alternatives.*
>
> *Abstract: [insert abstract here]*
>
> *Title: [insert title here]*

You can use any explicit delimiter (single, double, or triple quotes; tags; etc.) to help the query and AI along, and do not doubt your intent. While using delimiters might not make a difference in the output quality for straightforward tasks such as these, the more complex a task is, the more critical it is to disambiguate task details. Don't make the model work to understand precisely what you ask of them.

Tactic: Specify the steps required to complete a task

Some tasks are best specified as a sequence of steps. Writing the steps out explicitly can make it easier for the model to follow them.

Prompt:

> *Use the following step-by-step instructions to respond to my inputs for this and succeeding prompts:*
>
> *Step 1 - I will provide text in triple quotes. Summarize this text in one sentence with a "Summary: "prefix.*
>
> *Step 2 - Translate the summary from Step 1 into Spanish with a prefix that says "Translation: "*
>
> *"""insert text here"""*

Tactic: Provide examples

Providing ChatGPT with *general instructions* that apply to all examples is generally more efficient than *demonstrating all permutations* of a task by example. However, in some cases, providing examples may be easier.

For example, if you intend for the model to copy a particular style of responding to your queries, which is difficult to describe explicitly. This is known as "few-shot" prompting.

Prompt:

> *Answer in a consistent style.*
>
> *For example:*
>
> *Me: Teach me about patience.*
>
> *ChatGPT: The river that carves the deepest valley flows from a modest spring; the grandest symphony originates from a single note; the most intricate tapestry begins with a solitary thread.*
>
> *Me: Teach me about the ocean.*
>
> *ChatGPT:*

(Note: The blank space after "ChatGPT:" is intentional.)

Here's an example response from ChatGPT:

> *The ocean, vast and mysterious, covers over 70% of our planet's surface. It is a realm of boundless beauty and power where life flourishes in unimaginable diversity. Its depths remain largely unexplored, hiding secrets that intrigue and inspire. The ocean's waves, relentless and soothing, remind us of the ebb and flow of life's challenges and joys. Just as the tides rise and fall, so too do our own experiences, teaching us the importance of adaptability and resilience.*

Tactic: Specify the desired length of the output

You can ask the model to produce outputs of a given target length. The targeted output length can be specified in the count of words, sentences, paragraphs, bullet points, etc. However, instructing the model to generate a specific number of words does not work with high precision. The model can more reliably generate outputs with a specific number of paragraphs or bullet points.

Prompt:

Summarize the text delimited by triple quotes in about 50 words.

"""insert text here"""

Prompt:

Summarize the text delimited by triple quotes in 2 paragraphs.

"""insert text here"""

Prompt:

Summarize the text delimited by triple quotes in 3 bullet points.

"""insert text here"""

Strategy 2. Provide reference text

Ever heard of stories about lawyers getting lazy and then caught using ChatGPT for their cases, forgetting (or not realizing to) verify, and thereby forever cementing their careers in infamy? Language models like ChatGPT are notorious for confidently inventing fake answers (hallucinations), especially when asked about obscure topics or even (ironically) for citations and URLs. In the same way a sheet of notes can help a student do better on a test, providing reference text to these models can help answer with fewer fabrications.

Tactics:

- Instruct the model to answer using a reference text
- Instruct the model to answer with citations from a reference text

Tactic: Instruct the model to answer using a reference text

If you can provide a model with trusted information relevant to the current query, then you can instruct the model to use the provided information to compose its answer.

Prompt:

> *[insert articles here, each delimited by triple quotes]*
>
> *Use the provided articles delimited by triple quotes to answer questions. If the answer cannot be found in the articles, write "I could not find an answer."*
>
> *Question: [insert question here]*

Take note of the last sentence in the instruction: "If the answer cannot be found in the articles, write "I could not find an answer." This may not necessarily be followed at all times, but explicitly pointing this out can be significant.

Note also that all models have limited context windows. While this is improving as the tech advances, think of it like a chatty friend who only watches the last few minutes of the conversation. It helps understand what's happening now but forgets earlier details.

Hence, we need some way to adjust the information relevant to the question being asked in a way that does not diminish or limit the effectiveness of the exercise. There are ways to work around this if the model chokes or tells you the message exceeds its limit, such as having the model summarize the articles first before prompting this tactic; using a larger version (such as moving to GPT-4 if you have a ChatGPT

Plus account and were using GPT-3.5 at the time, for example); or limiting the number of articles attached if doing that did not materially reduce its effectiveness.

Tactic: Instruct the model to answer with citations from a reference text

Suppose the input has been supplemented with relevant knowledge (such as source links or a PDF attachment about a specific subject the following questions will discuss). In that case, requesting that the model add citations to its answers is straightforward by referencing passages from provided documents. Note that citations in the output can be verified programmatically by string matching within the provided documents or manually with a "Find" command in a word processor or other verification methods.

Prompt:

> *You will be provided with a document delimited by triple quotes and a question. Your task is to answer the question using only the provided document and to cite the passage(s) of the document used to answer the question. If the document does not contain the information needed to answer this question, simply write: "Insufficient information." If an answer to the question is provided, it must be annotated with a citation. Use the following format to cite relevant passages ({"citation": ...}).*
>
> *"""[insert your document here, or attach a separate document]"""*
>
> *Question: [insert question here]*

Strategy 3. Split complex tasks into simpler subtasks

Just as it is good practice in software engineering to decompose a complex system into a set of modular components, the same is true of tasks submitted to a language model like ChatGPT. Complex tasks tend to have higher error rates than simpler tasks. But then, complex tasks can also be re-defined as a workflow of simpler, more straightforward tasks in which the outputs of earlier tasks are used to construct the inputs to later tasks.

Tactic: Use intent classification to identify the most relevant instructions for a user query

For tasks in which lots of independent sets of instructions are needed to handle different cases, it can be beneficial first to classify the query type and use that classification to determine which instructions are needed. This can be achieved by defining fixed categories and hardcoding instructions for handling tasks in a given category. This process can also be applied recursively to decompose a task into a sequence of stages, something more easily done programmatically (as utilized by developers using the API), but can still be implemented to great effect manually.

The advantage of this approach is that each query will contain only those instructions (prompts) required to perform the next stage of a task, which can result in lower error rates than using a single query to perform the whole task. This can also result in lower instances or prompt refusals from ChatGPT due to the length since larger prompts can reach or exceed the context window's limit.

Suppose, for example, that for a customer service application, queries could be usefully classified as follows:

Prompt:

You will be provided with customer service queries from my freelance customers after I give you the instructions below. Please classify the following customer service query into primary and secondary categories and strictly present the classification in a Markdown table format with these keys: primary and secondary. Use the provided categories and subcategories to categorize the query. Do this only after this instructional prompt in relation to each of the queries I will post from my clients afterward.

Instructions:

Classify each query into a primary category and a secondary category.

Primary categories: Billing, Technical Support, Account Management, or General Inquiry.

Billing secondary categories:

- *Unsubscribe or upgrade*
- *Add a payment method*
- *Explanation for charge*
- *Dispute a charge*

Technical Support secondary categories:

- *Troubleshooting*
- *Device compatibility*
- *Software updates*

Account Management secondary categories:

- *Password reset*
- *Update personal information*
- *Close account*
- *Account security*

General Inquiry secondary categories:

- *Product information*
- *Pricing*
- *Feedback*
- *Speak to a human*

ChatGPT:

Certainly! Please provide the customer service query from your freelance customers, and I will classify it into the primary and secondary categories using the instructions you provided. Once you provide the query, I will format the output in a Markdown table format with the keys: primary and secondary.

Prompt:

I need to get my internet working again.

ChatGPT:

Based on the provided customer service query, here's the classification in a Markdown table format:

Primary Category	Secondary Category
Technical Support	Troubleshooting

Based on the classification of the customer query, a set of more specific instructions can then be provided to handle the next steps. This can be made as the next prompt in this chain, or instructions could have been embedded in the previous instructions above.

This example seems elaborate, and your context may be different for the particular use case you have, but it is an example of the process that you can reduce or add to as you see fit and as necessary for your task at hand.

Tactic: Handling Long Conversations in ChatGPT

Q: How do you eat an elephant?

A: One bite at a time.

When using ChatGPT for lengthy conversations, it's important to manage the conversation effectively, as the model has a fixed context length. Here are some strategies for effectively handling long conversations by splitting and summarizing them to ensure a smooth interaction:

Splitting into Multiple Prompts

- If your conversation becomes too long, consider splitting it into multiple prompts or messages.
- Each prompt should focus on a specific topic or question to organize the conversation.
- Start a new prompt when the context window is about to be exceeded to maintain context and coherence.

Summarize Previous Dialogue

- Instead of including the entire conversation in the context, summarize relevant parts.
- When the input reaches a certain length, you can trigger a prompt summarizing earlier conversation parts.
- Include the summary of the prior conversation as part of the next prompt.

Select Relevant Content

- Choose which parts of the conversation are most relevant to the current query.
- Include only the necessary context to maintain a concise and contextually relevant conversation.

Divide and Conquer: Summarize Long Documents Piecewise

- For highly long documents or texts, use a sequence of queries to summarize each section or segment.
- Concatenate section summaries to create a summary of summaries.
- This recursive process can be used until you've summarized the entire document.
- If earlier sections are needed to understand later sections, include a running summary of the preceding text while summarizing content at each point.

The main ideas are **compartmentalize requests, recap context, pare down to key details**, and **decompose bigger tasks**. With thoughtful prompting, you can stretch any chatbot's capabilities!

Strategy 4. Give the model time to "think"

OpenAI's guide notes: "If asked to multiply 17 by 28, you might not know it instantly, but you can still work it out with time. Similarly, models make more reasoning errors when answering right away rather than taking time to find an answer. Asking for a "chain of thought" before an answer can help the model reason its way toward correct answers more reliably."

In the same way that people give up way too easily when a language model responds suboptimally (particularly for tricky questions to the free version of ChatGPT), people forget that humans are susceptible to the same issues when you don't provide enough context or clarity in phrasing your inquiry. If you noticed as a common theme in this chapter as well as the OpenAI and similar guides, breaking down a concept and helping the language model "get" your intent is not just the computer's job, but yours. So make this consideration, particularly on more involved requests, and enjoy better output.

Tactic: Instruct the model to work out its own solution before rushing to a conclusion

Sometimes, models produce better results when we let them take time to reason through a problem before rushing to a conclusion.

For example, suppose we ask a model to evaluate a student's solution to a math problem. Rather than immediately asking if the solution is correct, it helps first to prompt the model to work through the problem itself.

Let's use the very same example OpenAI makes in its prompting guide (adjusted for a consumer's context; link to the source below):

Example (With erroneous answer first)

Prompt:

> *Determine if the student's solution is correct or not.*
>
> *Problem Statement: I'm building a solar power installation and need help working out the financials.*
>
> - *Land costs $100 / square foot*
> - *I can buy solar panels for $250 / square foot*
> - *I negotiated a contract for maintenance that will cost me a flat $100k per year and an additional $10 / square foot*
>
> *What is the total cost for the first year of operations as a function of the number of square feet?*
>
> *Student's Solution: Let x be the size of the installation in square feet.*
>
> 1. *Land cost: 100x*
> 2. *Solar panel cost: 250x*
> 3. *Maintenance cost: 100,000 + 100x*
>
> *Total cost: 100x + 250x + 100,000 + 100x = 450x + 100,000*

ChatGPT:

> *The student's solution is correct.*

That seems all well and good, except that the student's solution is wrong.

We can get the model to notice this by telling it to generate its solutions first.

Prompt:

> *First, work out your solution to the problem. Then, compare your solution to the student's solution and evaluate if the student's solution is correct or not. Don't decide if the student's solution is correct until you have done the problem yourself.*

Problem Statement: I'm building a solar power installation and need help working out the financials.

- *Land costs $100 / square foot*
- *I can buy solar panels for $250 / square foot*
- *I negotiated a contract for maintenance that will cost me a flat $100k per year and an additional $10 / square foot*

What is the total cost for the first year of operations as a function of the number of square feet?

Student's Solution: Let x be the size of the installation in square feet.

1. *Land cost: 100x*
2. *Solar panel cost: 250x*
3. *Maintenance cost: 100,000 + 100x*

Total cost: 100x + 250x + 100,000 + 100x = 450x + 100,000

ChatGPT:

Let x be the size of the installation in square feet.

1. *Land cost: 100x*
2. *Solar panel cost: 250x*
3. *Maintenance cost: 100,000 + 10x*

Total cost: 100x + 250x + 100,000 + 10x = 360x + 100,000

The student's solution is incorrect. They made an error in the maintenance cost calculation, using 100x instead of 10x. The correct total cost for the first year of operations is 360x + 100,000.

(Source: https://platform.openai.com/docs/guides/prompt-engineering/strategy-give-models-time-to-think)

These examples demonstrate that having the model work through the math itself first can better critically evaluate the student's solution rather than just guessing or making assumptions. This technique of prompting critical thinking ahead of assessments can result in more accurate and thoughtful responses.

Tactic: Ask the model if it missed anything on previous passes

When asking ChatGPT complex questions, it may not cover every relevant detail in its initial response. However, you can prompt the system to provide additional information by asking follow-up questions.

For example, say you ask the following open-ended question:

Prompt:

What key innovations allowed artificial intelligence to advance in the 2010s?

ChatGPT may respond with one or two major innovations in its first answer. You could then ask:

Prompt:

Please reflect. What other important AI innovations occurred in the 2010s that you did not already mention?

This cues ChatGPT to scan its own response, dig deeper into its knowledge, and find relevant details it may have initially omitted.

You may have also noticed in the above example that it is being asked to make a reflection, and the benefit of explicitly asking ChatGPT to reflect is to encourage it to think critically about a topic or provide a more thoughtful and considered response, potentially leading to a deeper and more insightful conversation.

The system can also be encouraged to elaborate on a specific point from its previous answer.

For example:

Prompt:

> *Are there more examples of relevant innovations? You mentioned advances in deep learning. Can you expand on the key breakthroughs in deep neural networks in that decade?*

In this way, you can engage ChatGPT in a dialogue to uncover fuller, more comprehensive responses to complex topics. Think of asking good follow-up questions as a *collaboration* with the system - together, you can construct the complete picture.

Conclusion

We explored the immense power and potential of ChatGPT, waiting to be unlocked through thoughtful, prompt design. Like a sculptor carefully chiseling stone, we shape ChatGPT's capabilities via the prompts we provide. Small tweaks can elicit dramatically different results.

We covered core strategies, from clearly specifying desired formats to asking targeted follow-up questions. While not exhaustive, consider this a starter kit of proven tactics to enhance your ChatGPT interactions immediately.

But the real craft comes with experimentation. Each conversation with ChatGPT as an opportunity for artful inquiry and playful prompts that inch us collectively closer toward beneficial outcomes. After all, mastery lies not in memorizing tactics but in tailoring and blending principles adaptively through spirited trial and error. So make these prompts your own - hack them, reshape them, try wild new permutations, and push boundaries. Use your creativity, intuition, and ethical judgment as the guiding light.

Key Takeaways

- Specify the desired output format, length, etc., in prompts

- Use delimiters, step-by-step instructions, and examples to disambiguate
- Provide reference texts for more accurate, contextual answers
- Ask follow-up questions to uncover more comprehensive responses
- Decompose complex tasks into sequences of more straightforward prompts
- Let the model reason through problems before rushing to conclusions
- Check if the model missed anything; ask for additional relevant details

Action Steps

- Use the prompts here as inspiration to try your variations
- Tailor and blend principles, test wild new prompt permutations
- Track results to determine optimal prompts for critical use cases
- Build a library of effective prompts for frequent queries

BONUS CHAPTER 3
HARNESSING THE POWER OF GPT-4 VISION

"Vision is the art of seeing what is invisible to others."

— Jonathan Swift

Imagine trying to learn how to swim, drive, or ride a bike by only reading a book. It will get you somewhere, but it would also be akin to watching your favorite movie in audio-only. With GPT-4 Vision, AI upgraded from text to multimedia, finally allowing it to see and visually interpret the world (and your question's real intent).

This chapter will explore how this new computer vision gives ChatGPT supercharged abilities to understand images, like turning a curious child loose in a world previously narrated only in words! We'll cover everything from how to access GPT-4 Vision to real-world applications, where it could narrate animal memes, interpret Uncle Larry's weird tattoo, or realize scribbles on a napkin into fully functioning websites.

Understanding GPT-4 Vision

Imagine telling a story to someone who can only hear but not see. They'll get the gist but miss out on the nuances a picture can provide. That's the leap from GPT-4 to GPT-4 Vision. GPT-4 Vision can "see" and understand images by integrating visual processing, adding a new dimension to AI interactions. It's like going from a radio show to a TV broadcast, where AI can now enjoy the whole story, pictures included.

This ability allows for a richer, more detailed understanding of queries involving images.

Evolution from GPT-4 to GPT-4 Vision:

GPT-4 was like a bookworm scholar who had read every book in the library but never gone outside to play. With GPT-4 Vision, it's like that scholar finally got recess privileges and can see and explore the schoolyard, unaware of the bullies that await but still opening up a whole new world of possibilities! This transition marks a significant advancement in AI capabilities, blending text and image processing. Initially, GPT-4 could only process text, like reading a book without pictures. GPT-4 Vision adds the "pictures" to the "book" and more besides, making the AI's responses more informative and contextually richer. It's a leap from understanding words to interpreting the world.

This foundational upgrade to GPT-4's capabilities sets the stage for exploring its practical applications and highlighting the significant advancement GPT-4 Vision represents in AI technology, moving from text-only interactions to a more holistic understanding and opening a whole new basket of tools through multimodal inputs.

Accessing and Using GPT-4 Vision

Access to GPT-4 Vision is currently available to ChatGPT Plus subscribers, so it's like getting a ticket to an exclusive concert, except that (most of the time) the tickets don't run out. So, if you haven't already, think of it like a premium subscription to your favorite streaming service. For a monthly fee (around $20 and above), you get (among others) access to the advanced features of GPT-4 Vision, turning your regular ChatGPT experience into one where you get a tool you can show anything, and it will tell or talk to you about it.

Let's break down the process of accessing and using GPT-4 Vision into simple, easy-to-follow steps, ensuring even those new to AI can confidently navigate and utilize this technology.

Accessing GPT-4 Vision

- Sign Up: First, create an account on OpenAI's platform, just like signing up for a social media account.

- Subscription Upgrade: Navigate to the "Upgrade to Plus" (or one of its other subscription tiers) section, then follow the process to complete. Think of it like choosing a better seat at a theater for a better view.

- Select GPT-4 Model: In your chat interface, select GPT-4 as your model – think of it as choosing the right lens for your camera. And voila, GPT-4 Vision is ready for use.

- Uploading Images: If you've done something as simple as attaching files via email or uploading an image to a social media post, you've already got this one in the bag. Uploading a photo is as easy as sending your AI assistant a selfie to analyze. It couldn't be simpler (unless the computer started responding with its selfies; then you'd either be impressed or run for the hills). Click on the image icon to upload your image.

- Crafting Prompts: Add a text prompt to guide the AI, like giving directions to a friend.

- Interpreting Responses: The AI will respond based on your image and prompt. It's like conversing, where you see and discuss the same picture.

Some of the Capabilities of GPT-4 Vision

Visual Inputs and Their Interpretation

GPT-4 Vision treats images like a detective at a crime scene, scrutinizing every detail. Whether it's a family photo, a historical document, or a complex chart, the AI examines it, understanding context and content. It's not just about seeing; it's about interpreting and making sense of colors, shapes, and text.

Let's explore how GPT-4 Vision can interpret and analyze visual information, showcasing its versatility and depth in understanding images.

Object Detection and Analysis

Imagine GPT-4 Vision as a toddler in one of those 'I Spy' games, except this toddler is freakishly good at it. It can instantly spot that needle in the haystack, find that teacup cat hiding in the cluttered room, identify a rare plant in a garden photo, or interpret the ghostly orb as the long-lost grand uncle hand-signaling from the afterlife (just kidding about that last one, but then you never know). But it's more than just naming objects; it offers insights about them, like a knowledgeable guide in a museum the size of the Earth, with almost everything in it.

Data Analysis from Visual Formats

Charts and graphs can be puzzling, but GPT-4 Vision reads them like experts. Like a seasoned analyst, it can look at a business graph and comment on trends, turning complex data into understandable insights, eyeballing graphs, and charts with the experience of a veteran financial analyst pouring over spreadsheets after reading a book on speed reading.

Text Deciphering in Images

Ever tried to read scribbled notes or faded text in an old book? GPT-4 Vision does that with confidence. It reads text within images, deciphering everything from a quick handwritten note to the fine print in a legal document. (Officially, ChatGPT may or may not fulfill this due to security and legal risks. But as known from various versions, this is a fact.)

Real-World Applications

Let's pick a few examples from an incredible array of possibilities available, demonstrating how GPT-4 Vision's capabilities can be applied in real-world scenarios and illustrating its versatility and impact across different industries.

Academic Research with GPT-4 Vision

GPT-4 Vision can help identify, clarify, contextualize, interpret, and provide insight on various applications.

Example: Imagine a historian researching medieval Europe trying to decipher an ancient faded manuscript, its text barely legible. She uploads an image of this manuscript to GPT-4 Vision, and voila! The AI reads the text and identifies the historical context, providing an interpretation and noting that the manuscript details a significant historical event. It's like having a time-traveling assistant who can read ancient scripts. All without needing a DeLorean or a flux capacitor.

Web Development - From Image to Code

GPT-4 Vision can transform a doodle of a website layout into actual HTML code. Say you casually sketch a precise drawing of your website idea on a napkin, upload it, and bam! GPT-4 Vision interprets your doodles and codes a fully functioning website faster than you can slowly pronounce "cascading style sheets."

This is one of the first demos OpenAI demonstrated about GPT-4 Vision; people are doing this today. It's like showing a sketch to a builder, who then constructs the building without much in-between (but also there for all the in-between you wish if that is what you want.)

Example: Consider a freelance web designer who sketches a website layout for a local bakery. They upload this sketch to GPT-4 Vision, which interprets the design and generates HTML and CSS code. The designer then tweaks the code to add personal touches. In hours, a functional and aesthetically pleasing website comes to life, saving days of coding work.

Data Interpretation and Analysis

Present GPT-4 Vision with a complex graph, and it will narrate the story behind the data. It's like a data whisperer, turning lines and bars into insights about market trends or population growth.

Example: A marketing analyst uploads a complex sales graph to GPT-4 Vision. The AI examines trends and provides insights like, "There's a consistent rise in sales every July, possibly due to seasonal marketing strategies." This information helps the marketing team in planning their next campaign.

Creative Content Creation

GPT-4 Vision aids in creative endeavors, too. For instance, in social media marketing to help generate ideas and visuals based on a theme, making it an invaluable tool for content creators.

Example: A social media manager wants to create a campaign about sustainable living. They feed GPT-4 Vision images of nature and urban settings. The AI generates ideas for posts, suggesting juxtapositions of nature and urban elements to highlight the importance of green spaces in cities.

More Examples

Let's make a quick run on various niches just to show the potential and versatility of examples, even as this also only barely scratches the surface.

Healthcare and Medicine

Example: A user notices a strange lesion in her right arm. She takes a picture from her smartphone and uploads it to GPT-4 Vision. After the usual caveats of the AI not being a doctor or expressing the benefits of getting professional help, it discusses what it sees in the image and spits out a list of possibilities. It may not officially make a diagnosis, but it can be a significant help in getting you to a better understanding of what's going on.

Numerous instances have emerged wherein ordinary folks have complemented their consultations with physicians by incorporating insights from GPT-4 and GPT-4 Vision. These reports encompass numerous cases of individuals who, having sought second and even third opinions from medical professionals, remained perplexed by the health issues they were experiencing, and after engaging in a series of conversations with ChatGPT, a more precise understanding (or better, such as nailing the exact disease) of the primary problem was eventually achieved, providing valuable assistance to these individuals.

Engineering and Product Design

Example: An engineer uploads a CAD design for a new consumer product, noting its various elements and details. GPT-4 Vision performs a critical assessment, notes points the engineer may have overlooked, and suggests structural integrity, aerodynamics, and ergonomics. It provides feedback to optimize the design before physical prototypes are created.

Scientific Research

Example: A marine biologist uploads images of a new deep-sea creature specimen collected from a recent exploration. GPT-4 Vision examines the photographs from multiple angles, compares physiological traits to other known species, and either suggests a classification within the Tree of Life or exposes the image to be of a known species but just taken from a distorted camera or angle.

Education

Example: A teacher uploads a diagram from a chapter in a history textbook about ancient civilizations. GPT-4 Vision interprets the visual components, generates explanatory captions and annotations, and creates supplementary quiz questions to boost student engagement.

Journalism and Media

Example: A photojournalist covering a public protest uploads images captured on the scene. GPT-4 Vision identifies key landmarks, interprets crowd expressions and signs to infer purpose, and cross-references visual details with previous events to provide historical context. Note that this example may require tiptoe-ing through security and privacy nightmares, but when done correctly, it can clearly benefit journalists and their audience.

Practical Prompt Engineering for GPT-4 Vision

Having reached this far into the book, you know that practical prompt engineering is like giving precise instructions to a talented but literal-minded genius. You need to be clear, specific, and creative to enhance the quality of responses and get the best results, crafting queries that guide ChatGPT to deliver the desired outcome. Like asking a genie for a wish: the more specific you are, the closer the result matches your expectations.

Prompting GPT-4 Vision is no different from the best practices of prompting in general, and while the inclusion of vision capabilities makes for whole new abilities, at its base, what you need to remember is not too different, and let me emphasize it for effect:

- **Be Specific**: If you want to know about a building in a photo, don't just ask, "What is this?" Instead, try, "Can you provide architectural details about this building?"
- **Provide Context**: If analyzing a graph, instead of asking, "What does this show?" say, "Can you analyze sales trends in this graph from 2010 to 2020?"
- **Sequence Your Queries**: Start with broad questions and then narrow them down. For instance, begin with "What objects are in this image?" and then ask, "What can you tell me about the vase on the table?"

More Examples

- For a historical photo: "Identify the era of the clothing styles in this photograph and provide historical context."
- For a medical chart: "Explain the trends in this patient's blood pressure readings over the past year."
- For a hand-drawn design: "Translate this sketch into a potential website layout, specifying design elements."

Limitations and Ethical Considerations

Understanding the Limitations

GPT-4 Vision isn't infallible despite its impressive capabilities. It can sometimes misinterpret images or miss nuances. It's like a well-read scholar who occasionally misunderstands a foreign idiom. Users should be aware of potential inaccuracies and use the tool as an aid, not the sole decision-maker. But don't let that diminish the impressive nature of what it is capable.

Navigating Ethical Concerns and Bias

Bias in AI is like unintended seasoning in a recipe; it can alter the flavor of the outcome. GPT-4 Vision may unintentionally perpetuate biases present in its training data. Users must recognize these biases and critically assess the AI's responses.

Best Practices for Responsible Use:

- Privacy First: Be cautious about uploading sensitive images. It's like not sharing personal diary entries publicly.
- Double-Check Facts: Always verify important information derived from GPT-4 Vision, as one would cross-reference facts from a single source.
- Avoid High-Risk Use: Refrain from using GPT-4 Vision for critical decisions in healthcare, legal, and safety-critical domains. It's not a replacement for professional expertise.

Exploring the Future of GPT-4 Vision and Multimodal AI

The future of GPT-4 Vision is intrinsically tied to the broader trend of multimodal AI, which combines multiple types of data input, like text, images, and even audio and video, in the future. This integration heralds a future where AI can provide more holistic and context-rich analyses.

AI's understanding and applications are as rich and varied as human perception. The immense potential of multimodal AI, exemplified by GPT-4 Vision, shows why Hollywood got it wrong. Many of its technologies slated for the 28th century are already here; the rest are on the way.

Tying Multimodal Trends with Future Developments

The future of GPT-4 Vision could be as intriguing as a sci-fi movie plot. We might see advancements where the AI can understand images in motion, akin to interpreting videos. Imagine GPT-4 Vision analyzing a movie scene and discussing cinematography. There could be improved accuracy in object and pattern recognition, making it more reliable in various professional fields.

As multimodal AI evolves, we might see GPT-4 Vision becoming capable of interpreting dynamic content such as videos or real-time imagery. This could revolutionize fields like remote learning, where AI could offer live commentary and explanations on educational videos and video interactions with students.

Imagining New Use Cases

The potential applications of GPT-4 Vision are vast. In education, it could help visually impaired students understand graphical content. In environmental science, it could analyze satellite images to track climate change effects. The potential and use cases are endless.

Converging text, images, and audio-visual data opens up unprecedented possibilities. For instance, multimodal AI could analyze patient records alongside diagnostic images in healthcare for more comprehensive care. Urban planning could evaluate architectural designs against environmental impact studies to suggest sustainable solutions.

GPT-4 Vision can already scrutinize cat memes and critically analyze an emotional drama scene, providing its review and ratings like the best of the film critics; so we're already living in the future, and you can just imagine what further awesome awaits, even though the future versions will yet likely surprise us some more.

Conclusion

We're standing at the threshold of a new era in AI capabilities. GPT-4 Vision's ability to process and interpret visual data and its text-based prowess offer a glimpse into a future where AI can interact with the world more human-like and have many exciting results of multimodally following along with it.

This chapter aimed to demystify GPT-4 Vision for everyday users, providing insights into its functionalities, practical applications, and ethical considerations. We've seen how it can be a powerful tool in various domains, from academic research to creative industries, while understanding the importance of responsible usage.

The journey into the world of multimodal AI is just beginning, and GPT-4 Vision is a significant step forward. There's much to explore and discover as users and creators, and the possibilities are as vast as our imagination or, better yet, as vast as AI's expanding and improving imagination.

Key Takeaways

- GPT-4 Vision integrates visual data processing with text, allowing AI to interpret images alongside text queries.
- Accessible to ChatGPT Plus and Enterprise users, it involves simple steps for uploading images and crafting effective prompts.
- Real-World Applications: GPT-4 Vision has diverse applications in academic research, web development, data analysis, creative content creation, etc.
- Effective communication with GPT-4 Vision at its core is no different from good prompting practices and requires specific, context-rich, and sequentially structured prompts.
- Despite its advancements, GPT-4 Vision has limitations in accuracy and potential biases, necessitating responsible and ethical usage.
- GPT-4 Vision represents a step towards more holistic AI interactions, combining multiple data types and modalities for richer analyses and interactions.

Action Steps

- **Explore GPT-4 Vision**: If you haven't already, sign up for ChatGPT Plus, familiarize yourself with the platform, and experiment with image uploads and prompts.
- **Apply in Your Field**: Identify how GPT-4 Vision can enhance your work or hobbies, whether in research, content creation, or data analysis.
- **Stay Informed**: Keep up-to-date with the latest developments in GPT-4 Vision and multimodal AI technologies.

Assignments

- Experiment with Different Prompts: Try various prompts with GPT-4 Vision to understand how specific queries yield different results.
- Analyze an Image: Choose an image relevant to your interest and use GPT-4 Vision to analyze it, noting its insights.

- Compare and Contrast: Use GPT-4 Vision on two similar images and compare the AI's interpretation and analysis of both.

Exercises

- Find the Object: Upload an image with multiple objects and ask GPT-4 Vision to identify a specific item.
- Historical Analysis: Upload a historical image and ask GPT-4 Vision to provide context or background information.
- Creative Captioning: Use GPT-4 Vision to generate a creative caption for a photograph.
- Data Interpretation: Upload a graph or chart and ask GPT-4 Vision to explain the trends or data shown.
- Web Design Conversion: Sketch a basic web page layout, upload it, and ask GPT-4 Vision to suggest (provide) HTML/CSS code.

Answers to Exercises (with Specific Prompts)

Find the Object:

- Example Prompt: "Identify and describe the blue vase in this image."
- Expected Answer: GPT-4 Vision should pinpoint the blue vase and provide a brief description or context.

Historical Analysis:

- Example Prompt: "Provide historical background for the building shown in this image."
- Expected Answer: The AI should offer historical information about the building, such as its age, architectural style, or significance.

Creative Captioning:

- Example Prompt: "Create a creative and humorous caption for this image."

- Expected Answer: GPT-4 Vision should generate a relevant caption that adds a creative or humorous twist to the image.

Data Interpretation:

- Example Prompt: "Explain the key trends in this sales graph from 2015 to 2020."
- Expected Answer: The AI should interpret the graph, outlining major sales trends and notable changes over the specified years.

Web Design Conversion:

- Example Prompt: "Convert this sketch into a basic web page layout, suggesting HTML and CSS structures."
- Expected Answer: GPT-4 Vision should translate the sketch into a basic web page design, providing suggestions for HTML and CSS code.

PROMPTING DALL-E 3

"The aim of art is to represent not the outward appearance
of things, but their inward significance."

— Aristotle

Introduction

DALL-E 3 is an artificial intelligence system created by OpenAI to generate images from text prompts ("text-to-image"). It learned to visually interpret language descriptions by analyzing vast datasets connecting text captions with corresponding images. Earlier versions, while groundbreaking, faced challenges such as image distortion and lower resolution, which have been progressively addressed in subsequent updates.

DALL-E 3 represents an exponential leap in AI's artistic capabilities, and as good as it became and continues to improve, it had gotten arguably infinitely better not by its own inherent abilities (for which it has plenty) but because it was integrated into ChatGPT and is now a seamless part of it.

This chapter will explore how proper prompting is key to unlocking this tool's immense potential for creators and innovators. When fueled by human imagination, DALL-E 3's ability to give visual form to our most fantastic ideas is incredibly empowering. This chapter will show you how to take the DALL-E 3 bull by the horns and properly steer this versatile canvas so you can enjoy the many wonders it places at your fingertips.

How DALL-E 3 Works

OpenAI developed DALL-E 3 to generate realistic images from text prompts. The model gained the ability to link language and visuals through training on large datasets of image-text pairs.

When you enter a prompt, DALL-E 3 analyzes the words to comprehend key objects, styles, and details desired in the image. Advanced AI processes attempt to interpret prompts similarly to human understanding.

DALL-E 3 leverages complex deep-learning capabilities to synthesize the described scene, and a systematic, layer-by-layer procedure selects shapes, colors, lighting, and compositions to match prompts.

Unlike diffusion-based models, DALL-E 3 utilizes a transformer architecture for image generation. OpenAI continuously refines DALL-E, with major updates achieving milestones like enhanced realism. Recent versions focused on accurately rendering finer details, coherently arranging elements, and improving fidelity in producing aesthetically and contextually accurate images. A growing brilliance belying how it's maturing enough to translate text into imagery convincingly reflects the immense number of visual patterns it has learned and the exceptional improvements it promises.

The Art of Crafting DALL-E Prompts

The key to unlocking DALL-E's potential lies in understanding how to speak its language - prompts. Every nuance and descriptive phrase influences the nature of the images generated, making prompt engineering an impactful skill for ChatGPT and all aspects of AI, including DALL-E.

Let's break down the key components that comprise effective prompts:

221

Subject/Focus

The main subject or focus of the image. This is best described unambiguously through concrete nouns - e.g., "owl," "fruit basket," and "the Eiffel Tower." Defining a clear subject provides an anchor for DALL-E to render details around.

Style

The aesthetic style, art genre, era, or other qualities modify the subject's rendition. Examples include "photorealistic," "impressionist," "abstract," "cubist," or specifying a time period. Stylistic elements create cohesion.

Modifiers

Additional descriptors add nuance to lighting, angle, ambiance, and emotion. For example, "dramatic side-lighting," "quizzical gaze," and "lush grass in the background." Modifiers elevate basic prompts through the atmosphere.

Creative Liberties

This involves taking an initial prompt foundation and adding an unexpected twist - merging concepts across disciplines fancifully. Like visualizing "a cactus in the shape of a penguin for a product shot of a grooming kit for men" or "a fruit basket castle." Such creative liberties depend on solid prompt bases to then subvert.

When combined effectively, these elements enable DALL-E to render surprisingly focused images. However, balance is also vital - overloading prompts with too many details can sometimes lead to less coherent outputs. Aim for clarity while allowing room for interpretation.

Now let's look at some key techniques for wielding prompt components skillfully, and you'll see that it isn't very different from prompting

ChatGPT in general and does not deviate from general prompting best practices:

- **Use concrete, unambiguous terms**

  DALL-E understands direct, literal descriptions much better than vague or abstract ideas. Using concrete nouns and adjectives leaves less room for interpretation - focusing on DALL-E's image generation. Say "a red bird" instead of "a bird," for example.

- **Leverage datasets it was trained on**

  Many of DALL-E's visual learnings are derived from real-world photos and artwork. Prompts related to its training corpora, like natural scenes, portraits, or common objects, often produce higher-quality results.

- **Build off proven base prompts**

  Start with simple prompts that reliably generate coherent images for you, then incrementally add modifiers and creative elements to these bases. E.g., beginning with "a still life painting of fruit" and then tweaking styles.

- **Apply a structured composition**

  Organize prompts into subject, style, and modifiers, e.g., "A woman in a gown, oil painting, dramatic chiaroscuro lighting style." This composition helps DALL-E balance attention across prompt aspects.

- **Use creative and emotional modifiers**

  Phrases like "triumphant pose," "curious gaze," "lush grass," or "ethereal lighting" can elicit more inspired, evocative images from DALL-E by suggesting ambiance.

The prompts we compose become the boundaries for DALL-E's artistic interpretation. We can direct it with mindful phrasing and structuring to fulfill both pragmatic and creative goals.

It's also worth noting that while DALL-E can approximate different artistic styles, the accuracy of replication depends on what it has learned from its training data. Outcomes may vary.

Now that we have grasped DALL-E's prompt system let's survey special modifiers that can transform results.

Prompt Modifiers and Their Influence

Beyond fundamental prompt components, DALL-E displaying creative flair stems from the artful use of modifiers - descriptive words and phrases suggesting desired attributes. Modifiers act as "seasoning" for prompts - bringing emotive qualities, lighting ambiance, and more into the generative process.

When applying modifiers, balance creative expressiveness with practical feasibility. Let the core prompt provide a grounding structure, then artfully season as appropriate for the context. Not all flavors suit all dishes.

Let's explore some common prompt modifiers and their impact on DALL-E 3 outputs:

Lighting and Ambience

Cues like:

- "Sunrise lighting"
- "Cinematic ambiance"
- "Moonlit scene"

These suggest specific illumination context to DALL-E - influencing the time of day, intensity, and mood depicted. Lighting can spotlight subjects or set an alluring ambiance.

Emotion and Personification

Cues like:

- "Triumphant pose"
- "Pensive gaze"
- "Whimsical abstraction"

Emotion modifiers inject feeling and personalities into depictions of people, animals, or anthropomorphic subjects - as if bringing still images to life through implied narrative.

Detail and Focus

Cues like:

- "Ultra-high resolution"
- "Shallow depth of field"
- "Fine details"

These emphasize precision rendering in aspects like sharpness, depth of field for focus fall-off, and intricacy of textures/designs.

Angle and Perspective

Cues like:

- "Worms-eye view"
- "Isometric angle"
- "Fish-eye lens"

Such modifiers let us dictate vantage points and camera lens effects to control scene perspectives and composition dynamism.

Artistic Style

Cues like:

- "Cubist style"

- "Surrealist"
- "Hanna Barbera cartoon"

As noted above, while DALL-E can approximate different artistic styles through relevant modifiers, the accuracy of style replication depends on what visual concepts it has learned from its training data, so outcomes may vary in matching the desired style, and knowing this eliminates surprises.

This illustrates how modifiers expand possible outcomes. But like other best practices, it's important to remember to use them judiciously rather than overloading prompts.

For example, we can shift whole image aesthetics into different genres and eras through historical art periods or pop culture stylistic references.

The key is using modifiers judiciously rather than overloading prompts. A compelling image demands enough meaningful details to imply depth, lighting to set the tone, and a focal point for coherence. With experimentation, you'll eventually discover which modifiers best emphasize the essence of specific subject matters.

Practical Applications in Various Fields

Now that we understand DALL-E fundamentals let's survey professional use cases harnessing its imagery for enhanced outcomes across niches, industries, and sectors:

Marketing and Advertising

DALL-E is a game-changer for attention-grabbing graphic content. Consider:

- Stylized product photos adapted across campaigns
- Envisioning branding assets and environments
- Conceptual images conveying emotions and narratives

Entertainment: Film, Books, Music

Great for visual ideation like:

- Novel cover artwork conveying genres/themes
- Concept art for characters and scene settings
- Promotional graphics with band/artist themes

Education

Useful for illustrating educational concepts through:

- Textbook diagrams explaining complex processes
- Infographics clarifying abstract ideas
- Adaptable anatomy and nature drawings

Architecture and Design

DALL-E accelerates design workflows via:

- Interior space visualizations with various furnishings/styles
- Quick home decor concept iterations
- Product renderings to evaluate shape and materiality

Engineering and Manufacturing

Support prototyping by

- Testing CAD models under varied simulated conditions
- Generating photorealistic renderings of products early on
- Exploring stylistic variations on product designs

These use cases will continue expanding as DALL-E's capabilities grow over time.

The core advantage is producing high volumes of customizable images without extensive manual effort - saving creators time while inspiring new ideas.

However, while DALL-E has recently made a huge leap, it currently faces some limitations, such as generating text within images or maintaining consistency in sequential images. As the technology continues progressing, more specialized applications may become more feasible.

Common Pitfalls and How to Avoid Them

While DALL-E empowers impressive results, specific prompt issues can undermine outcomes. Being aware of these pitfalls allows tweaking inputs to avoid problems. Let's outline frequent areas of difficulty and their remedies:

Ambiguous Terms

Using vague language often produces incoherent images in DALL-E. Descriptors come across as too open-ended to visualize concretely.

For example, prompting for simply a "bird" could generate almost any avian species in unpredictable poses. But asking for a "scarlet macaw flying mid-air" focuses on rendering specificity through deliberate details.

When image results seem confusing or variable, ensure prompts use unambiguous terms. Especially when DALL-E has high fidelity to prompts, especially relative to its competition.

Unrealistic Combinations

DALL-E allows mashing up disparate concepts, but not all combinations align sensibly. Attempting overly esoteric blends like "business suit armor" strains its efforts at coherent visualization.

Keep imaginative prompts grounded in compatible styles and eras and have logical connections. For example, "sleek futuristic robotic armor" visually blends sci-fi technology with body protection and may seem ridiculous, but makes sense.

Replicating Work by Many Artists

While DALL-E can generate images in various artistic styles, it does not replicate the work of specific artists, especially contemporary or modern artists who are still protected by copyright laws.

Missing Structural Prompt Elements

Sometimes, generated images appear disjointed because certain prompt fundamentals are overlooked. For instance, solely describing a "dramatic sky" and omitting surroundings and context risks odd elements such as floating backgrounds or simply unintended results.

Revisiting the "subject, style, modifier" prompt formula safeguards the inclusion of crucial bounding elements. Here, specifying perhaps "wolf howling at a dramatic sky" stages a concrete scenario.

Ignoring AI Bias

People sometimes forget that AI isn't human (yet) and that ChatGPT is a tool, so we must remain mindful that AI systems like DALL-E may inadvertently reproduce biases in their training data. Like ChatGPT, you must be mindful of the ethical considerations and potential biases in AI-generated images, especially in sensitive applications. Creating images responsibly requires thoughtful consideration of ethical issues and cultural sensitivity. We must apply the same care to crafting inclusive, respectful prompts as creative ones.

As DALL-E evolves, we must continuously learn and adapt our prompting practices. Ethical questioning is an ongoing exercise as new capabilities emerge. With DALL-E's flexibility comes an obligation to question the technology's potential consequences through prompts - ensuring that imagination and progress are fueled responsibly.

Prompting Strategies

For beginners, it's important to master fundamental single prompt techniques before attempting intricate sequences.

As your prompt crafting intuition grows, more advanced techniques open up creative possibilities.

Seeding

This involves taking an existing DALL-E-generated image and incorporating it into a new prompt to derive extended versions. (This is not the now-deprecated seeding concept that appears to have been replaced with the gen_id method described below.

For example, imagine fantasizing about an "astronaut playing chess with an alien" and then using that image to seed an evolution like an "oil painting of an astronaut playing chess with an alien in a meadow."

Generation/Image ID

Inside a session, you can create better-matched, consistent image results by referring to the image generation ID (**gen_id**) and passing that as the *refering_image_id*.

DALL-E now assigns a unique generation ID (gen ID) to each image it creates, and can often capture stylistic elements and preferences.

To view the gen ID, ask ChatGPT to "Show me the generation ID of the last image." Then, to create a new image with a similar style or preferences, use the *referenced_images_ids* parameter in a new prompt, providing the gen ID as a reference.

Here's an example to illustrate the concept:

1. Generate the Initial Image

Prompt:

Create a photorealistic painting of a cat wearing a spacesuit.

2. Retrieve the Gen ID

Prompt:

Show me the generation ID of the last image.

It will respond with a unique string of characters representing the gen ID (e.g., "abc123xyz").

3. Construct a New Prompt

Compose a new prompt for a different image, incorporating the referenced_images_ids parameter and setting it to the retrieved gen ID.

Prompt:

Create a photorealistic painting of a dog playing chess, using referenced_images_ids = ["abc123xyz"].

DALL-E will then generate an image aiming to capture the style and preferences from the initial image while adhering to the new prompt's content requirements.

While gen IDs can't guarantee exact replication of a previous image, they can produce images with similar stylistic elements.

Chaining

Building prompt sequences that connect images, guiding DALL-E through narrative visualizations.

It begins with "a taxi driver staring pensively out the car window at night in the rain," then chaining prompts leading through an imagined story, as described in the prompting strategies of the preceding chapters.

Assisted Art Directing

Provide an initial prompt, review results, then refine inputs to shift outputs towards a target creative vision incrementally. Almost collaborating with DALL-E through rounds of direction, response, and guidance steps - ultimately achieving your imagined and intended (or happily accidental-) outcomes.

While these tactics can enhance creativity, they also require a strong grasp of how DALL-E interprets prompts to avoid unintended outcomes. Start simple before attempting intricate sequences.

We've covered core principles - now let's envision the future, noting the speculative nature of these AI predictions.

Future Trends and Developments

AI image generation is progressing swiftly, with models like DALL-E 3 demonstrating enormous creative potential already. However, certain coherence, reasoning, and user control limitations still constrain its capabilities.

By contemplating likely horizons of advancement, we can map out how prompting might evolve (while noting caveats like the speculative nature of AI predictions like this):

Increasing Coherence Across Longer Prompts

While DALL-E interprets initial prompt segments reliably, coherence sometimes breaks down over lengthy or complex descriptive chains. Future training focused on contextual understanding between prompt elements promises a more robust handling of intricate imaginative prompts.

Intuitive Handling of Atypical Concepts

Today, even well-formed prompts like "an astronaut playing chess with an alien" might strain credible visualization and performance. But models are learning faster assimilation of non-standard combinations through exposure to ever broader datasets alongside improving theories beyond training. Soon, less familiar blends will be reconciled smoothly into better image outputs through training.

Enhanced User Shaping of Creative Directives

Rather than sole text, future interfaces could allow direct "painting" of desired atmosphere, style, or layout cues. Models like DALL-E would interpret these creative directions on the fly during image formulation. Mixed modal inputs beyond just typed phrases may direct outcomes more intuitively.

Conclusion

Our journey into DALL-E prompting has illuminated foundational techniques and creative frontiers. We can guide this infinitely imaginative artist by understanding its visual language patterns.

DALL-E's magic arises from combining computational power with human imagination through prompts, and as the technology's grasp over imagery and aesthetics matures, so too will the artistry continue to blossom.

However, it is important we remain cautiously optimistic - actual developments are unpredictable and may diverge from expectations as the field continues to evolve rapidly, so it's important to keep up-to-date with the latest advancements. By sustainably advancing AI through transparency and ethical questioning, we pave the way for realizing benefits responsibly and effectively.

Key Takeaways

- DALL-E is based on a transformer architecture, but the field is evolving, and new models or approaches might be added or in use at any time
- Like prompting ChatGPT in general, the same goes for DALL-E: well-structured prompts provide clarity for DALL-E and yield superior results
- Modifiers add emotive depth and personalized style
- Check common pitfalls to refine the quality continuously
- Creativity excels when grounded in practicality
- This technology remains constantly evolving

Action Steps

- Catalog a library of reliable base prompts
- Maintain an inspiration list for modifier combinations
- Bookmark your favorite generated images to seed future prompts

- Practice iteratively art directing DALL-E to outcomes
- Responsibly share your vibrant visions with the world

Exercises

1. Generate a magazine cover displaying an uplifting message
2. Create an infographic mockup explaining prompt engineering fundamentals
3. Visualize a fantastic creature that blends multiple animals

Answers to Exercises

Magazine cover with an uplifting message

- Prompt: "A glitzy, high-fashion magazine showing modern visuals and a photo of a supermodel, with happy people behind her, as they leisurely talk in a verdant landscape, conveying a message of hope."

Infographic mockup on prompt engineering

- Prompt: "A colorful infographic poster explaining key concepts in crafting prompts for AI image generation in flat design"

Fantastic creature blend

- Prompt: "Create an image of an underwater fantasy creature with the head of a horse, the body of a dolphin, the tentacles of an octopus, and wings like a manta ray"

LEAVE A REVIEW

Thank you so much for purchasing my book and for making it all the way to the end!

Before you go, I wanted to ask you for one small favor. Could you please consider posting a review on the platform? Posting a review is the best and easiest way to support the work of independent authors like me.

If you enjoyed d this book, I'd really appreciate it if you left your honest feedback. I love hearing from my readers, and I personally read every single review.

Your feedback will help me to keep writing the kind of books that will help you get the results you want. It would mean a lot to me to hear from you.

Printed in Great Britain
by Amazon

38371297R00136